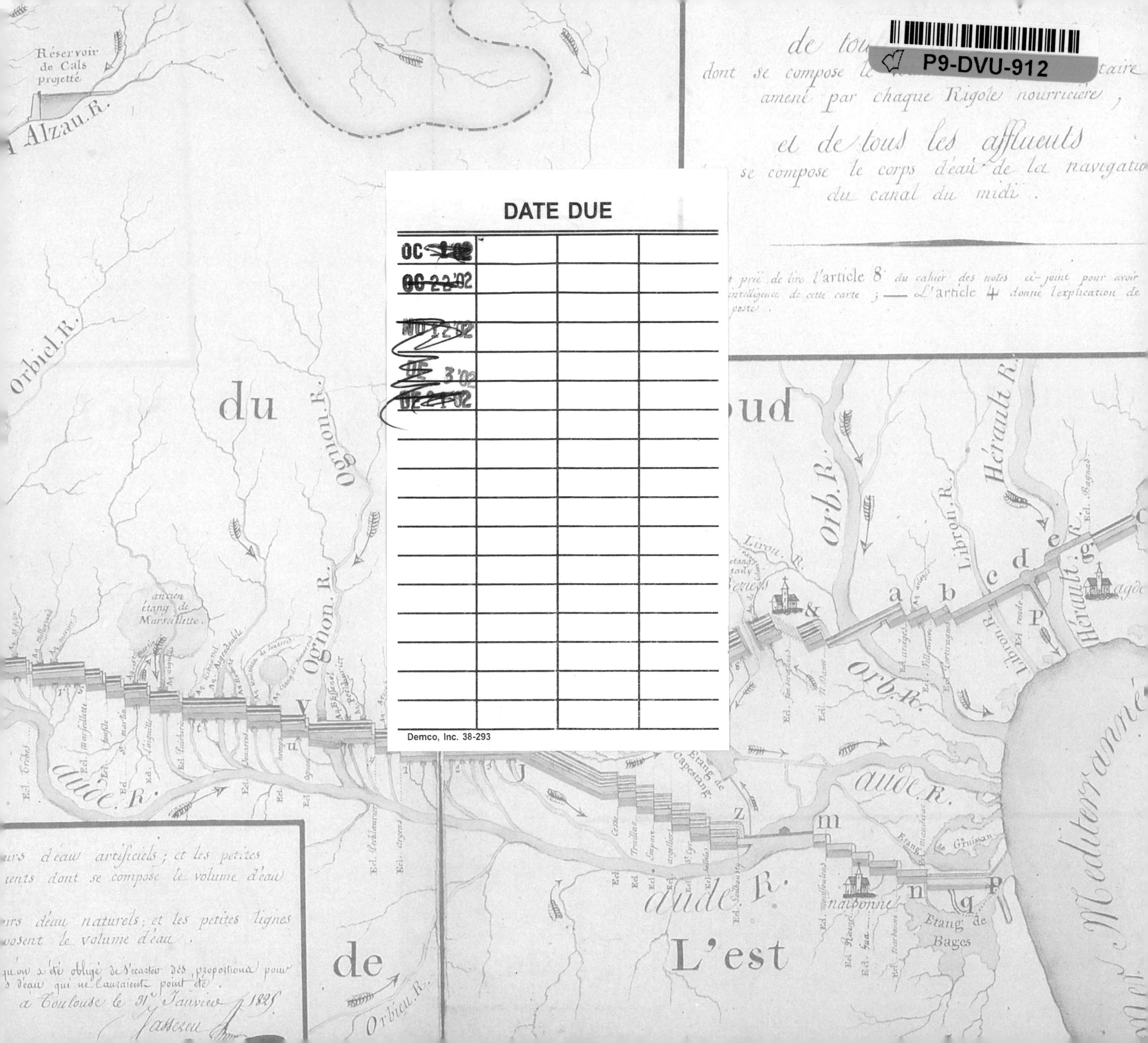

Réservoir de Cals projetté
Alzau. R.
dont se compose
amené par chaque Rigole nourricière,
et de tous les affluents
se compose le corps d'eau de la navigatio
du canal du midi.
L'article 8 du cahier des notes ci-joint pour avoir
intelligence de cette carte ; — L'article 4 donne l'explication de
Orbiel. R.
du
Ognon. R.
oud
Orb. R.
Libron. R.
Hérault. R.
ancien étang de Marseillette.
Béziers
aude. R.
Etang de Capestang
Etang de Gruissan
narbonne
Etang de Bages
Méditerranée
de
L'est
Orbieu. R.
urs d'eau artificiels ; et les petites
uents dont se compose le volume d'eau
urs d'eau naturels ; et les petites lignes
posent le volume d'eau.
à Toulouse le 31e Janvier 1825
DATE DUE
Demco, Inc. 38-293
P9-DVU-912

"I am now in the land of corn, wine, oil, and sunshine.
What more can man ask of heaven?
If I should happen to die at Paris I will
beg of you to send me here, and have me
exposed to the sun. I am sure it
will bring me to life again."

–Thomas Jefferson

Thomas Jefferson's JOURNEY TO THE SOUTH OF FRANCE

Roy & Alma Moore

INTRODUCTION BY
LUCIA C. STANTON
Shannon Senior Research Historian, Monticello

STEWART, TABORI & CHANG
NEW YORK

Published in 1999 by Stewart, Tabori & Chang
A division of U.S. Media Holdings, Inc.
115 West 18th Street, New York, NY 10011

Distributed in Canada by General Publishing Company Ltd.
30 Lesmill Road, Don Mills, Ontario, Canada M3B 2T6

Library of Congress Cataloging-in-Publication Data
Moore, Roy.
Thomas Jefferson's journey to the south of France / Roy & Alma Moore ; introduction by Lucia C. Stanton.
p. cm.
Includes bibliographical references (p.) .
ISBN 1-55670-892-0 (alk. paper)
1. Jefferson, Thomas, 1743-1826—Journeys—France, Southern. 2. France, Southern—Description and travel. 3. France, Southern--Pictorial works. I. Moore, Alma Chesnut. II. Jefferson, Thomas, 1743-1826. III. Title. IV. Title: Journey to the south of France.
E332.745.M66 1999
914.4'80435'092—dc21 98-32376
CIP

Printed in Hong Kong

10 9 8 7 6 5 4 3 2 1

First Printing

PREVIOUS PAGE: MINERVE

For Yvonne . . . her garden in Provence.

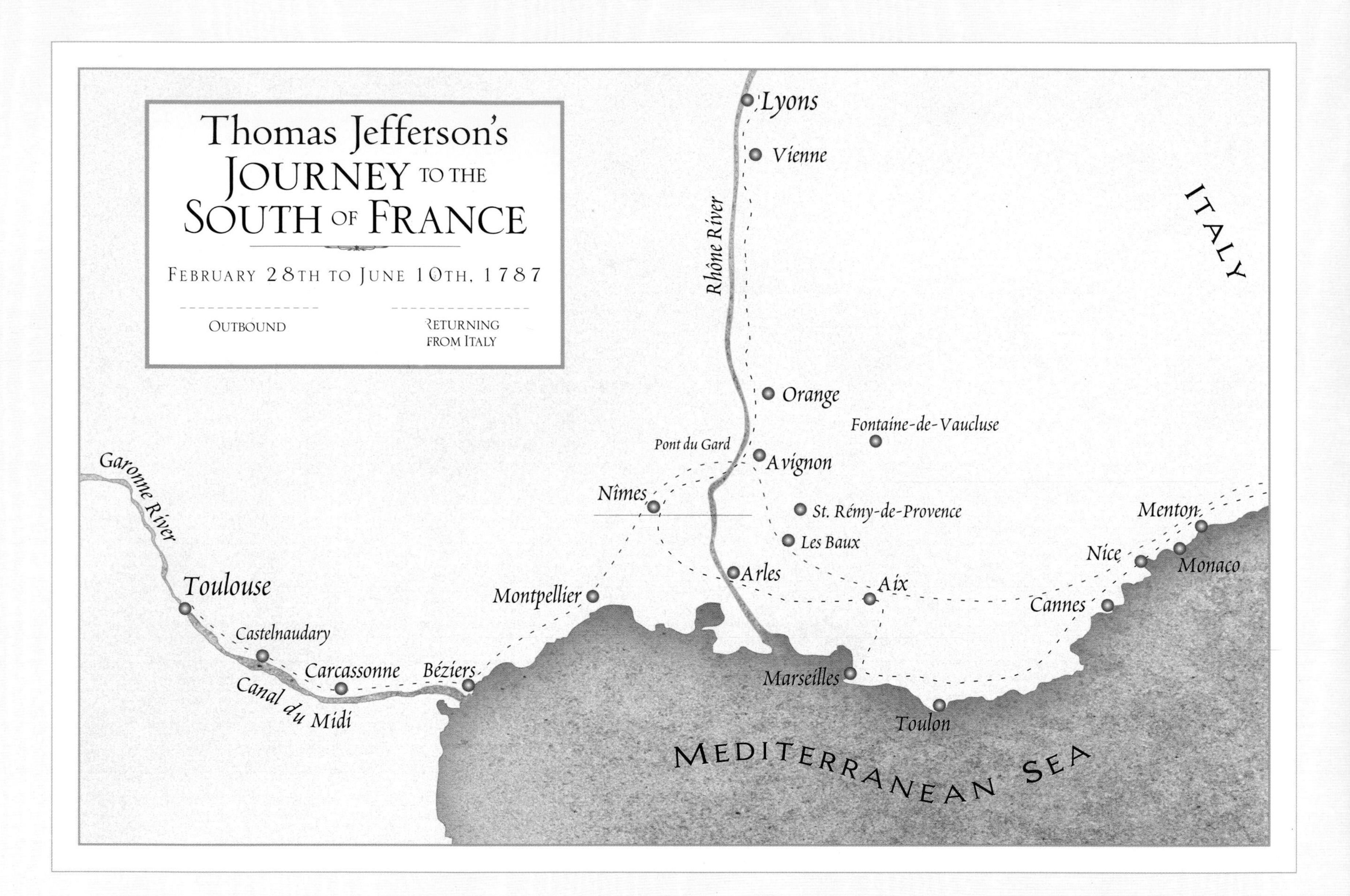
Thomas Jefferson's
JOURNEY TO THE
SOUTH OF FRANCE
FEBRUARY 28TH TO JUNE 10TH, 1787
OUTBOUND
RETURNING FROM ITALY
Lyons
Vienne
Rhône River
ITALY
Orange
Fontaine-de-Vaucluse
Pont du Gard
Avignon
Nîmes
St. Rémy-de-Provence
Les Baux
Garonne River
Toulouse
Arles
Aix
Montpellier
Menton
Nice
Monaco
Cannes
Castelnaudary
Carcassonne
Béziers
Canal du Midi
Marseilles
Toulon
MEDITERRANEAN SEA

Thomas Jefferson's Itinerary
Spring, 1787

FEB. 28 — *Set out from Paris*

MCH. 9 — *Château de Laye Epinaye*

MCH. 11 — *Lyons*

MCH. 15 — *Vienne*

MCH. 18 — *At Orange*

MCH. 19 — *Le Pont du Gard, Nîmes*

MCH. 24 — *At Arles, Tarascon, St.-Rémy*

MCH. 25 — *At Aix-en-Provence*

MCH. 29 — *Left Aix for Marseilles, the Riviera, and Nice*

APR. 10 — *At Nice*

APR. 13 — *Left Nice for Italy*

MAY 1 — *At Menton, Monaco, Nice*

MAY 3 — *At Aix*

MAY 8 — *At Avignon, Vaucluse*

MAY 9 — *At Villeneuve d'Avignon, Pont du Gard, Nîmes*

MAY 11 — *At Montpellier*

MAY 14 — *Embarked on the Canal de Languedoc*

MAY 15 — *At Béziers*

MAY 18 — *At Carcassonne*

MAY 19 — *At Castelnaudary*

MAY 21 — *At Toulouse and the end of the Canal de Languedoc*

MAY 24 — *Visit to Atlantic port cities*

JUNE 10 — *Return to Paris*

INTRODUCTION

BY LUCIA C. STANTON

The South of France, as the words on page one imply, cast its spell on Thomas Jefferson and induced a kind of resurrection of his spirit. Two and a half years amid the cultural riches of Paris had begun to dispel the pall of grief and indifferent health that enveloped him after the death of his wife, Martha, in 1782. In the fall of 1786, a few weeks of gallivanting across the French capital with the beautiful Maria Cosway provided a further tonic. But, two months later, he would still confess to a friend, "I am burning the candle of life without present pleasure, or future object." Then, in the spring of 1787, when he encountered the unbroken sunshine of the south, his depression evaporated along with some of his inhibitions. Jefferson's letters and journals from three months of travel reveal a rarely seen side of his personality. Seldom did he so fully disclose the poetic man of sensibility beneath the cloak of reason he habitually buttoned about himself.

He feasted his eyes on the colors of the landscape and the angles of Roman buildings, listened with delight to the music of birdsong and the Provençal language, inhaled the scents of lavender and thyme, and savored the regional food and wines at every stop. Words like "delicious," "superb," "sublime," "feast," and "rapture" flew from his pen as he recorded each new scene. The unbuttoned Jefferson was still recognizably rational, however. He could marvel at the beauty of a grove of olive trees, while pondering their utility to American citizens and monitoring their range as an indicator of climate. He relished a glass of Médoc as he ascertained the cost and methods of its production. When the nightingale captivated him in the season of its glory, he considered ways to "colonize" it in the United States. And, as he gazed lover-like at the ruins of Roman civilization, he took measurements of their bricks and arches.

For Jefferson, beauty and utility were bound together. "I am an enthusiast on the subject of the arts," he wrote James Madison a year after arriving in Paris, and he assessed the sights he saw against the concept of "utile dulci" ("the useful with the delightful") expressed by his favorite Roman poet, Horace. From his youth, Jefferson had fully absorbed the Enlightenment love of learning as well as a deep concern for its social benefits. He was happiest when his curiosity was guided by a larger national, or even universal, purpose—all part of what he later called his "zeal for improving the condition of human life."

On his southern tour, the American minister to the Court of Louis XVI was able to blend private concerns with a public mission. He could combine "instruction, amusement, and abstraction from business," as he expressed his personal aims, with an inspection of the state of Franco-American trade in the southern seaports and an examination of the renowned canal linking the Mediterranean with the Atlantic Ocean. Originally planned for the fall of 1786, the journey was first postponed when Jefferson dislocated his right wrist in a fall in September. Then, when the ministrations of surgeons and bonesetters failed to assuage his pain, he determined to undertake the trip in the winter in order to try the mineral waters of Aix-en-Provence. His multipurpose expedition was further delayed by diplomatic business and the opening of the Assembly of Notables.

Maria Cosway by Richard Cosway

Finally, on the last day of February, 1787, Jefferson was ready to depart. Leaving behind his fifteen-year-old daughter, Martha, a boarder in a Paris convent school, he headed south in his own carriage, traveling post. Every ten miles, at a posthouse, he paid for a fresh set of horses and another postilion, strikingly clad in blue and red uniform and outsized iron-bound jackboots. To the dismay of his friends, Jefferson began his journey without a servant, "quite determined to be master of my own secret." He meant to travel, not as American minister to France but as Thomas Jefferson, private citizen, so as not to "insulate" himself from the people. In Dijon, as "a sacrifice to opinion," he hired Petit Jean, who accompanied him for the remainder of the journey.

In the best Enlightenment spirit, Jefferson had fully equipped himself for productive travel. His baggage contained his portable copying machine, made to his own design in London, which pressed out the only surviving copies of some of his most delightful letters. He carried sheets of paper to record every sou of his expenditures, variations of climate, and daily jottings about his surroundings. He had also carefully assembled some suitable tools for an assiduous collector of useful information—a pocket thermometer and several tape measures ordered from London.

Thus armed with pen, thermometer, and measuring tape, Jefferson preserved for posterity an encyclopedic collection of information on agriculture, economy, climate, and culture that, in a fair copy made after the journey, covered forty-four pages. From Burgundy to Provence, along the Mediterranean to the plains of the Italian Piedmont, and back through Languedoc to the Atlantic coast, he made notes on the color of the soil, the price of bread and butter, the methods of vine cultivation, the shapes of plows and women's hats, the blooming of almond trees, and the singing of frogs. He recorded morning and afternoon temperatures from Nîmes to Toulon, where his thermometer apparently broke, and he drew forth his measuring tape to gauge the size of bridges and monuments, barrels and pumps, elder and orange trees, and even mules. Here is a sampling from the travel journal, unabridged:

> *March 25. 26. 27. 28. Aix...Dung costs 10s. the 100lb. Their fire wood is chene-vert and willow. The latter is lopped every three years. An ass sells for from 1. to 3. Louis; the best mules for 30. Louis. The best asses will carry 200. lb., the best horses 300 lb., the best mules 600 lb. The temperature of the mineral waters of Aix is 90.° of Farenheit's thermometer at the spout. A mule eats half as much as a horse.*

Jefferson's letters strike a different note. Seasoned with classical and literary allusions, they transformed the welter of detail in the journal into a sequence of resonant and colorful scenes that reveal the intensity of his engagement with both the landscape and its people. In the wine region of Burgundy, which he explored on horseback, he set the pattern for his investigations of the countryside, "going into the houses of the labourers, cellars of the Vignerons, and mixing and conversing with them as much as I could." He felt that the dinner hour, when he could see how the peasantry was fed, as well as clothed and housed, was best for discovering the influence of politics on the "happiness of the people." For three months in 1787, Jefferson was a patriotic pleasure-seeker, on the alert for gifts to take back to his countrymen—technological advances, new plants and animals, approved models in architecture, and fresh thoughts on political philosophy.

Jefferson left Paris on the road to Fontainebleau and, "pelted" with rain, hail, and snow, traveled as quickly as several carriage breakdowns allowed to Dijon and the vineyards of Burgundy. He hired a local wine-cooper and "a peasant" to accompany him to the most celebrated vineyards of Pommard, Volnay, Meursault, and Montrachet. He then passed into the Beaujolais, "the richest country I ever beheld," to pay a two-day visit at the Château de Laye Epinaye. While there he fell in love with "a delicious morsel of sculpture," a Diana and Endymion by René Michel Slodtz. He allotted four days to Lyon, where he paid for more carriage repairs, refreshed his cash supply, and visited a tailor. He saw some "good things" in painting and some "feeble remains" of antiquity—a theater and remnants of an aqueduct.

Roman remains became progressively less feeble as he rolled south, however. The monuments that had nourished his architectural imagination in black and white on the pages of books, he now could see in three dimensions and full color. He was chagrined to find the first full-fledged Roman structure of the trip—the temple of Augustus and Livia in Vienne—embellished with Gothic windows and in use as a church. He was consoled by the "handsome" pyramid in the same town and took out his measuring tape to examine this "inedited" monument (that is, not described in the scholarly literature). Mathematical accuracy was critical to an understanding of the proportions of classical architecture and thus to the expression of universal standards of beauty.

Roman fragments from Orange

After another ramble on horseback through the vineyards of the Côte Rôtie, Jefferson continued to follow the Rhône south to Tain-l'Hermitage. The landlord of the post-house, "a most unconscionable rascal," tested his philosophy of travel—never to judge national character by the propensity of postillions, waiters, and tavernkeepers for "pillaging strangers." But the vin du pays was captivating. He made the brisk climb among the vineyards to the top of the hill "impending" over the village for the sake of its "sublime prospect." And, fifteen years later, when he began making annual orders of white Hermitage as President, Jefferson called it "the first wine in the world without a single exception."

The "delicious" scenery in the vicinity of Montélimar was followed by the gateway to a world that had a wholly unexpected appeal. "Here begins the country of olives," Jefferson wrote at Pierrelatte, just north of Orange. The next three weeks, he told the Marquis de Lafayette, were "a continued rapture to me," and the olive tree was their leitmotif. He filled his journal with the olive's specifications and his letters with its virtues. He began tracing its appearance and disappearance, its size and health, its culture, and the manufacture of its oil. Astonished by the way it could thrive in the absence of tillable soil, he observed that its cultivation "gives being to whole villages." His enthusiasm for this new discovery reached its apogee in a three-page paean he composed on his return to Paris, punctuated with uncharacteristic exclamation points. "I never had my wishes so kindled for the introduction of any article of new culture into our own country," he told William Drayton of South Carolina. The prospect of the introduction of "the richest gift of heaven" to the American south assumed for him the dimension of a national duty. He arranged for several shipments of olive trees to Charleston and waited to hear of whole groves spreading across the south, ousting the unhealthful culture of rice, "which sows life and death with almost equal hand." Because of the season of his travel, Jefferson did not fully understand the weather of Provence, matched in the United States only in California. But what he unwittingly traced, in monitoring the olive's range while he scanned Les Alpilles from his carriage or viewed the Alpes Maritimes from the back of a mule, were the boundaries of the Mediterranean climate, as the olive is now recognized as marking its extent. Over a decade later, when he sat down to ask himself "whether my country is the better for my having lived at all," he made a list of his services to his nation, including his introduction of the olive alongside his sweeping revisal of the Virginia laws after the American Revolution. With thoughts of the spring of 1787 in his mind, he penned his famous statement, "The greatest service which can be rendered any country is to add an useful plant to its culture."

The Fountain of Nostradamus

Orange itself held the first "precious remains of antiquity" to excite his superlatives, the "sublime" arch and the "superb" Roman theater. He then crossed the Rhône on the celebrated thirteenth-century Pont St.-Esprit and took the road to Nîmes, instead of Aix, ostensibly to keep an appointment with a Brazilian revolutionary, but surely because he could not postpone his first meeting with the "most perfect and precious remain of antiquity in existence." Passing through "very romantic scenes," with a stop at the Pont du Gard, he reached Nîmes, where he observed the blooming apple trees and the first butterfly of the season, but spent most of his time gazing at the Maison Carrée "like a lover at his mistress." The object of his "passion" was the building that had already inspired his design for the Virginia state capitol.

From Nîmes he sent the first of his rhapsodic letters about the South of France. "I am immersed in antiquities from morning to night," he wrote to Adrienne-Catherine de Noailles, Comtesse de Tessé. "For me the city of Rome is actually existing in all the splendor of it's empire." The aunt of the Marquise de Lafayette, two years older than Jefferson, shared with him a love of "architecture, gardening, a warm sun, and a clear sky" that made her the natural recipient of his first effusions. Madame de Tessé and her husband had a Paris house on the Rue de Varenne but it was Chaville, their country residence near Versailles, that was her natural habitat. Jefferson had been enlisted in the project to provide American plants to the Chaville gardens and he recalled its "charming society" for the rest of his life. His letters to the Comtesse and her protégée Madame de Tott were probably consciously crafted for a wider circle, since he well knew her appetite for reading aloud. And, in fact, she replied that she had read his letter to their friends, "as, doubtless, they used to read those of the apostles at the gathering of the early Christians."

Jefferson spent four happy days at Nîmes, in the company of the Roman amphitheater and the Roman baths in the Jardin de la Fontaine, as well as the Maison Carrée. He filled the interludes of gazing at this monument by attending to the silk spinners and stocking weavers who populated the square. He bought thirty pairs of the "cheapest" silk stockings, had them embroidered with the date and his initials in the Roman fashion, "T.I.", and put them on his portable scales to weigh them to the nearest pennyweight. He also bought books and medals, perhaps from one of the "shabby antiquarians" who had approached Tobias Smollett twenty years before. These "cheats," Smollett wrote, sold "the vilest and most common trash" to the undiscerning, but brought out "some medals which are really valuable and curious" when they recognized a connoisseur.

Jefferson's route to Aix contained two more required stops for the lover of classical architecture. He viewed and measured the "fine" amphitheater at Arles, which, like that in Nîmes, was encrusted inside and out with dwellings and sheltered, as Jefferson heard, 1,000 inhabitants. At Saint-Rémy, he entered the landscape of van Gogh and Les Baux, the ruined city that is a major twentieth-century tourist destination but was of no interest to Jefferson. Instead, he made inquiries about alfalfa and olive trees and saw two monuments from the age of Augustus.

Finally, over three weeks after leaving Paris, he reached Aix-en-Provence. In four days he took forty douches in 90° water at the thermal establishment. Whether, as one contemporary phrased it, he "subjected his contracted limb to the stream" in the octagonal public room or hired one of the few private baths, the experiment was "without any sensible benefit" to his wrist. While he said there was "little to be seen" in Aix, he enjoyed its sunshine and was impressed by its cleanliness, which caused him to meditate on the political meaning of dung. He made arrangements for transporting some of the water of Aix to his first public destination, the port of Marseilles. Here he spent over a week investigating questions of American commerce, days as full of social activity as sightseeing and information gathering. He found it a "charming" place, "all life and activity," and entertained Madame de Tott with a playful soliloquy on the sounds of a Provençal city: the tinkling of the bells on the mules, the braying of 300 asses, and the squabbling of 4,351 market women.

From Marseilles he wrote to the Marquis de Chastellux that his trip had been "a continued feast of new objects, and new ideas...I have courted the society of gardeners, vignerons, coopers, farmers &c. and have devoted every moment of every day almost, to the business of enquiry." With all his interests working in unison, he looked into the effects of Algerian pirates on American shipping and made notes on firewood, the meals of mules, the price of beef, and the method of preserving figs. Although he never described one of his own meals, passing references to the flavor of mutton or the excellence of the bread and olive oil indicate that he was savoring the local cuisine. With the implications of the Assembly of Notables always in the back of his mind, he developed a routine for reading the politics of France in its landscape. As he expressed it to the Marquis de Lafayette, "You must ferret the people out of their hovels as I have done, look into their kettles, eat their bread, loll on their beds under pretense of resting yourself, but in fact to find if they are soft. You will feel a sublime pleasure in the course of this investigation, and a sublimer one hereafter when you shall be able to apply your knolege to the softening of their beds, or the throwing a morsel of meat into the kettle of vegetables."

Only the cause of Carolina rice drew Jefferson further east along what he deemed "little more than a rocky coast." His pleasure was undiminished, however, as he viewed botanical gardens and orange plantations in Toulon, Hyères, and Antibes. He paid customs at the Var River and crossed from France to the Kingdom of Sardinia, that is, Italy. His three days in Nice generated speculations about relative comfort and climate that foreshadowed the judgments of the tourists that would later come in a stream to the resorts of the Riviera. Jefferson compared Nice to Hyères and Marseilles and found its climate "quite as superb as it has been represented." On his birthday, April 13, he left Nice on the back of a mule, climbing up through the Maritime Alps. With several books on the subject of Hannibal's march to Rome in his baggage, he sought the trail of the Carthaginian general and his motley army of 70,000 mercenaries and 37 elephants. His daughter's letters of complaint about the difficulties of Livy's Latin had roused him to write her from Aix, "We are always equal to what we undertake with resolution." Similar thoughts must have occurred to him as he contemplated Livy's account of the army's struggles without roads, map, or compass, and Hannibal's famous exhortation to his reluctant troops: "No part of the earth is unclimbable by man."

Passing from Turin to Milan to Genoa, Jefferson learned that the machine for husking rice was "absolutely the same" as that in South Carolina. He filled his coat pockets with unhusked rice and engaged a muleteer to smuggle more to Genoa—acts that were, he was told, punishable by death. Architecture and gardens were primary concerns, as usual, and he spent a day, "from sunrise to sunset," observing the process of making Parmesan cheese. Just out of his reach were the lands of Palladio and the Roman republic; a two-week "peep only into Elysium" was all he had time for. He attempted the return from Genoa to Nice by sea, but contrary winds forced the felucca to shore, and he continued his journey, "clambering the cliffs of the Appennine, sometimes on foot, sometimes on a mule." Then he traveled westward for two days and nights, made brief stops in Aix and Marseilles, and finally slowed his pace again on May 8 at his next tourist destination.

Aix-en-Provence

Jefferson went to Avignon primarily as a literary pilgrim. Making no mention of the Palace of the Popes, he visited instead the simple tomb marking the grave of Petrarch's beloved Laura and made a happy excursion to the Fontaine de Vaucluse, famous as Petrarch's retreat for sixteen years. The powerful force of the emerging river and the picturesque ruins of Petrarch's "chateau," perched on a precipice above, gave an "enchantment" to the scene that was enhanced by finding "every tree and bush filled with nightingales in full chorus." Jefferson, who happened to have met the nightingale in the height of its song season, was inspired with thoughts of transporting this species to the United States. After another night in Nîmes and two days in Montpellier, he took to the water again at Sète.

The previous fall, Jefferson had expressed his "great desire to examine minutely" the Canal de Languedoc (today known as the Canal du Midi). Here was a seventeenth-century engineering marvel that could be of incomparable benefit to the new American nation. He probably never expected it would also provide "the pleasantest" mode of travel he ever experienced. After sailing across the Étang de Thau from Sète to Agde, he hired a private vessel to move at a more leisurely pace than the post boat to Toulouse. For nine days, he walked along the canal banks or observed the passing landscape from his dismounted carriage. Enjoying "cloudless skies above, limpid waters below," and a "double row of nightingales" in full song, he wrote from the canal one of the most lyrical letters of his journey to his daughter Martha, who until then had received mainly geography lessons and homilies on idleness.

Floating through Béziers, Carcassonne—about which he left no comment, and Castelnaudary, he examined the hundred locks along the way and made a day-long tour of the canal's feeder system of dams, tunnels, and a remarkable subterranean chamber, where, 160 feet beneath the reservoir, the guide opened the valves and Jefferson heard the thundering of torrents of water. In Toulouse on May 21, he tipped the captain and crew of his vessel and was back on the roads twenty-four hours later, his idyll in the south essentially over, even though he would be a tourist for three more weeks. He diligently visited the Atlantic ports of Bordeaux (also making a close examination of the surrounding vineyards), La Rochelle, and Lorient, stopped in Tours to puzzle over the apparent "spontaneous" growth of shells described by Voltaire, and saw two châteaux in the Loire Valley—the Duc de Choiseul's Chanteloup and Madame de Pompadour's Château de Ménars.

On June 10, a seventy-five-mile day, he arrived in Paris after three months of living in hotels, having covered "something upwards of a thousand leagues" in his carriage, on fifteen ferry boats and three larger vessels, and on the backs of various horses and mules. He was reunited with his daughter Martha—soon to be joined by her sister, Mary—and returned to weekly ceremonial visits to Versailles and a press of diplomatic business. But, for the rest of his life, he drew from an imagination charged with the sights, sounds, and tastes of his journey. He filled the Monticello cellars and wareroom with Provençal products, making annual orders of wine, almonds, artichoke hearts, capers, and olive oil—one of his "necessaries of life." He monitored the fate of his olive tree shipments and sowed Mediterranean crops, like madder and sainfoin, at Monticello. He offered his expertise on canals to enterprising Americans and, in his design of the University of Virginia, he used an architectural language enriched by the classical buildings he had examined along the Rhône.

Many contemporaries commented on Jefferson's frequent allusions to "the most agreeable country on earth," as he described France in 1814. As Secretary of State, he read aloud from his 1787 travel journal to Dr. Benjamin Rush and other friends. As President, he regaled John Quincy Adams with the tale of the Marseilles wine merchant who could blend cheap and perfect imitations of the finest claret, causing Adams to remark, "You can never be an hour in this man's company without something of the marvellous." Jefferson was known for turning presidential dinner conversation to topics of gardening and agriculture, injecting accounts of the figs of Marseilles and the oranges of Hyères. Near the end of his life, when he wrote, "I slumber without fear and review in my dreams the visions of antiquity," he must have seen in his mind the beautiful geometry of Roman stone in the sunlit olive groves of the South of France.

Right: St. Rémy

I am just setting out on a journey of three months to the South of France . . .

THOMAS JEFFERSON, LETTER TO ELIZA HOUSE TRIST, FEBRUARY, 1787

LEFT: HOTEL SULLY, PARIS.
RIGHT: JEFFERSON'S POCKET NOTEBOOKS, WHICH HE USED IN FRANCE, WERE MADE OF IVORY LEAVES. WHEN TRAVELING, HE WROTE NOTES IN PENCIL THAT COULD BE ERASED AFTER THEY WERE TRANSFERRED TO PAPER.

To Vergennes

Paris Feb. 11. 1787.

Sir
My hand recovering very slowly from the effects of it's dislocation, I am advised by the Surgeons to try the waters of Aix in Provence. From thence I think it possible I may go as far as Nice. As circumstances might arise under which a passport might be useful, I take the liberty of troubling your Excellency for one. I propose to set out on Thursday next.

I would at the same time ask an enfranchisement for three barriques of common wine, and one of wine de liqueur, one of which is arrived at Paris, and the other three are soon expected there. They are for my own use.

With my sincere prayers for the speedy reestablishment of your health, I have the honor to assure you of those sentiments of perfect esteem & respect with which I am your Excellency's most obedient and most humble servant,

Th: Jefferson

Left: Louvre
right: Paris arcade

To Madame de Tott

Paris Feb. 28. 1787.

Have you been, Madam, to see the superb picture now exhibiting in the rue Ste. Nicaise, No. 9. chez Mde. Drouay? It is that of Marius in the moment when the souldier [ente]rs to assassinate him. It is made by her son, a student at Rome under the care of David, and is much in David's manner. All Paris is running to see it, and really it appears to me to have extraordinary merit. It fixed me like a statue a quarter of an hour, or half an hour, I do [not] know which, for I lost all ideas of time, "even the consciousness of my existence." If you have not been, let me engage you to go, for I think it will give you pleasure. Write to me your judgment on it: it will serve to rectify my own, which as I have told you is a bad one, and needs a guide. It will multiply too the occasions of my hearing from you; occasions which I claim by promise, and which will strew some roses in the lengthy road I am to travel. That your road, through life, may be covered with roses, is the sincere prayer of him who has the honour to mingle his Adieus with sentiments of the most affectionate esteem and respect,

Th: Jefferson

Window façade, Louvre

To Madame de Tessé

Paris Feb. 28. 1787.

If you will be so good, Madam, as to send to my hotel any letters with which you will be pleased to honour and relieve me on my journey, Mr. Short if he is here will take care to forward them, and with the more care as coming from you. If he should not be here, they will be forwarded by a servant who has charge of the house. My letters will be sent to me by post twice a week.

...I set out on my journey in the moment of writing this. It is a moment of powerful sensibility for your goodness and friendship, wherein I feel how precious they are to my heart, and with how affectionate an esteem & respect I have the honor to be Madam, your most obedient & humble servant,

Th: Jefferson

From Martha Jefferson

Panthemont february
[i.e., March] 8

Being disapointed in my expectation of receiving a letter from my dear papa, I have resolved to break so painful a silence by giving you an example that I hope you will follow, particularly as you know how much pleasure your letters give me. I hope your wrist is better and I am inclined to think that your voyage is rather for your pleasure than for your health. However I hope it will answer both purposes. I will now tell you how I go on with my masters. I have began a beautiful tune with balbastre, done a very pretty landskip with Pariseau, a little man playing on the violin, and began another beautiful landskape. I go on very slowly with my *tite live*, its being in such ancient italian that I can not read with out my master and very little with him even. As for the dansing master I intend to leave him off as soon as my month is finished. Tell me if you are still determined that I shall dine at the abesse's table. If you are I shall at the end of my quarter. The kings speach and that of the eveque de Narbone has been copied all over the convent. As for Monseur he rose up to speak but sat down again with out daring to open his lips. I know no news but supose Mr. Short will write you enough for him and me too. Mde. Thaubenen desires her compliments to you. Adieu my dear papa. I am afraid you will not be able to read my scrawl, but I have not the time of coppying it over again. Therefore I must beg your indulgence and assure [you] of the tender affection of yours,

M Jefferson

Pray write often and long letters.

Above: Miniature of Martha Jefferson by Joseph Boze
Right: Garden of the Musée Cluny
Following page: Hillside in the South of France

Château de Laye Epinaye

After passing through the Beaune and Burgundy countryside, Jefferson stopped for three days at the Château de Laye Epinaye, built in 1740. He was the guest of the Comtesse de Laye, whose husband was away at the time. Jefferson admired the chateau and its surrounding landscape. He inspected the vineyards and farms and tasted the local wines. Legend has it that he copied the pattern of an elegant floor in one of the reception rooms, which he later used for the parlor floor at Monticello. Having rested his horses and repaired his carriage, he proceeded, by way of Lyons, to Vienne.

LEFT: CHÂTEAU DE LAYE EPINAYE

This is the richest country I ever beheld.

CHÂTEAU DE LAYE EPINAYE. The face of the country is like that from Chalons to Macon. The Plains are a dark rich loam, the hills a red loam, of midling quality, mixed generally with more or less coarse sand and grit, and a great deal of small stone. Very little forest. The vineyards are mostly inclosed with dry stone wall. A few small cattle and sheep. Here, as in Burgundy, the cattle are all white.

This is the richest country I ever beheld. It is about 10. or 12. leagues in length, and 3. 4. or 5. in breadth; at least that part of it which is under the eye of the traveller. It extends from the top of a ridge of mountains running parallel with the Saone, and sloping down to the plains of that river scarcely any where too steep for the plough. The whole is thick sown with farm houses, chateaux, and the Bastides of the inhabitants of Lyons. The people live separately, and not in villages....The wages of a labouring man here are 5. Louis, of a woman one half. The women do not work with the hough: they only weed the vines, the corn, &c. and spin. They speak a Patois very difficult to understand. I passed some time at the Château de Laye Epinaye. Monsieur de Laye has a seignory of about 15,000 arpens, in pasture, corn, vines, and wood. He has over this, as is usual, a certain jurisdiction both criminal and civil. ...—M. de Laye has a Diana and Endymion, a very superior morsel of sculpture by Michael Angelo Slodtz, done in 1740. The wild gooseberry is in leaf, the wild pear and sweet briar in bud.

THOMAS JEFFERSON,
Notes of a Tour into the Southern Parts of France, &c.

RIGHT: DRAWING ENTITLED "VUE DU CHÂTEAU ST. DENIS ESPINAY." THE CHÂTEAU IS DEDICATED TO ST. DENIS AS IS THE CHAPEL. JEFFERSON KNEW IT AS THE CHÂTEAU DE LAYE EPINAYE.

VUE DU CHATEAU S^T. DENIS ESPINAY, DÉP^T. DU RHÔNE.
PRO FIDE
PRO REGE
PRO ME
VIRTUTE
NOBILITAS
ILLUSTRATUR
(1) S.A.R. Mad^me la Duchesse de Berry.

Vienne

The roads from Lyons to St. Rambert are neither paved nor gravelled. After that they are coated with broken flint. The ferry boats on the Rhone, and the Isere, are moved by the stream, and very rapidly. On each side of the river is a moveable stage, one end of which is on an axle and two wheels, which, according to the tide, can be advanced or withdrawn so as to apply to the gunwale of a boat. The Pretorian palace at Vienne is 44. feet wide, of the Corinthian order, 4. columns in front, and 4. in flank.

THOMAS JEFFERSON,
Notes of a Tour into the
Southern Parts of France, &c.

LEFT AND ABOVE: THE TEMPLE OF AUGUSTUS AND LIVIA—BUILT IN 26 BC AND RESTORED IN 1865—IS A SMALLER VERSION OF THE MAISON CARRÉE AT NÎMES, WHICH WAS CONSTRUCTED MORE THAN A CENTURY LATER. TODAY, DESPITE THE ENCROACHMENT OF HOUSES AND VARIOUS COMMERCIAL ENTERPRISES, IT IS ONE OF THE MOST ATTRACTIVE REMAINS OF THE ROMAN OCCUPATION.

To William Short

Lyons Mar. 15. 1787.

Dear Sir
So far all is well. No complaints; except against the weathermaker, who has pelted me with rain, hail, and snow, almost from the moment of my departure to my arrival here. Now and then a few gleamings of sunshine to chear me by the way. Such is this life: and such too will be the next, if there be another, and we may judge of the future by the past. My road led me about 60 miles through Champagne, mostly a corn country, lying in large hills of the colour and size of those in the neighborhood of Elkhill. The plains of the Yonne are of the same colour, that is to say, a brownish red; a singular circumstance to me, as our plains on the water side are always black or grey. The people here were ill clothed, and looked ill, and I observed the women performing the heavy labours of husbandry; an unequivocal

proof of extreme poverty. In Burgundy and Beaujolois they do only light work in the feilds, being principally occupied within doors. In these counties they were well clothed and appeared to be well fed. Here the hills become mountains, larger than those of Champagne, more abrupt, more red and stony. I passed thro about 180 miles of Burgundy; it resembles extremely our red mountainous country, but is rather more stony, all in corn and vine. I mounted a bidet, put a peasant on another and rambled thro' their most celebrated vineyards, going into the houses of the labourers, cellars of the Vignerons, and mixing and conversing with them as much as I could. The same in Beaujolois, where nature has spread it's richest gifts in profusion. On the right we had fine mountain sides lying in easy slopes, in corn and vine, and on the left the rich extensive plains of the Saone in corn and pasture.

This is the richest country I ever beheld. I passed some time at the Chateau de Laye Epinaye, a seignory of about 15,000 acres, in vine, corn, pasture and wood, a rich and beautiful scene. I was entertained by Madame de Laye with a hospitality, a goodness and an ease which was charming, and left her with regret. I beg of you to present to the good Abbés Chalut and Arnoud my thanks for their introduction to this family: indeed I should be obliged to you if you could see Monsr. de Laye and express to him how sensible I am of my obligation to him for the letter to Madame de Laye, and of her attention and civilities. I have been much indebted here too for the letters from the Abbés, tho' the shortness of my stay does not give me time to avail myself of all their effect. A constant tempest confined me to the house the first day: the second, I determined to see every thing within my plan before delivering my letters, that I might do as much, in as little time, as possible. The third and fourth have been filled up with all the attentions they would admit, and I am now on the wing, as soon as this letter is closed. I enter into these details because they are necessary to justify me to the Abbés for the little time I had left to profit of the good dispositions of their friends. Six or seven hundred leagues still before me, and circumscribed in time, I am obliged to hasten my movements. I have not visited at all the manufactures of this place: because a knowlege of them would be useless, and would extrude from the memory other things more worth retaining. Architecture, painting, sculpture, antiquities, agriculture, the condition of the labouring poor fill all my moments. Hitherto I have derived as much satisfaction and even delight from my journey as I could propose to myself. The plan of having servants who know nothing of me, places me perfectly at my ease. I intended to have taken a new one at every principal city, to have carried him on to serve me on the road to the next and there changed him. But the one I brought forward from Dijon is so good a one that I expect to keep him through the greater part of the journey, taking additionally a valet de place wherever I stay a day or two. You shall hear from me from Aix where I hope to meet letters from you giving me news both great and small. Present me affectionately to my friends and more particularly to Madame de Tessé and Madame de Tott: and accept assurances of my perfect esteem & friendship to yourself. Adieu.

Th: Jefferson

Orange

Having spent two days investigating the vineyards and vintages of the Tain region, Jefferson visited Orange, the site of a great Roman victory. He seemed fascinated by the "sublime Triumphal Arch," which was built in 21-26 AD to commemorate the victories of Rome's Second Legion. Jefferson then visited Orange's most famous ruin, "the superb theater" whose outer wall, 338 feet long and 118 feet high, was described by Louis XIV as the "finest wall in the Kingdom."

Above: Inner wall of the Roman Theater, Orange
right: Outer wall

Right: Triumphal Arch and Theater, Orange, painted by Hubert Robert in 1787, the same year Jefferson visited the site. Left: Photograph of the Triumphal Arch as it appears today.

Thyme growing wild here on the hills

MAR. 18. PRINCIPALITY OF ORANGE....Here begins the country of olives, there being very few till we enter this principality. They are the only tree which I see planted among vines. Thyme growing wild here on the hills. Asses very small, sell here for 2. or 3. Louis. The high hills in Dauphiné are covered with snow. The remains of the Roman aqueduct are of brick. A fine peice of Mosaic, still on it's bed, forming the floor of a cellar. 20 feet of it still visible. They are taking down the circular wall of the Amphitheatre to pave a road.

THOMAS JEFFERSON,
Notes of a Tour into the Southern Parts of France, &c.

Le Pont du Gard

On his way to Nîmes, Jefferson stopped to view the magnificent Pont du Gard, situated in a countryside of olive trees and wild vegetation, which was constructed by Agrippa in 19 BC to carry water from Uzès to Nîmes, twenty-five miles away. Where the aqueduct crossed the Gardon River, the Romans created what Jefferson called "this sublime antiquity." Transporting forty-four million gallons of water per day, Le Pont du Gard was constructed without mortar, the varying courses held together with iron clamps.

LEFT: PONT DU GARD PAINTED BY HUBERT ROBERT
OVERLEAF: A VIEW OF THE PONT DU GARD TODAY.

Wild figs, very flourishing, grow out of the joints of the Pont du Gard...

THOMAS JEFFERSON,
Notes of a Tour into the Southern Parts of France, &c.

Scale 1 square = 1'
Virginia Capitol: End elevation - Study

Nîmes

In Nîmes, Jefferson hurried to see "the most perfect model of antient architecture remaining on earth...." The Maison Carrée, built in the first century, was so lovely that Colbert, Louis XIV's minister, wanted it moved to Versailles. Showing a strong Greek influence, the Maison Carrée was used by Jefferson and Clerisseau, his friend and architect, as the model for the Virginia State Capitol building in Richmond, Virginia. Jefferson also visited the Temple of Diana in the Jardin de la Fontaine. The amphitheater, slightly smaller than the one in Arles, was built in 50 AD and is the best preserved in existence. Due to its intricate and cleverly built stairways and galleries, more than twenty thousand people could exit the arena in mere minutes.

Left: Sketch of the front elevation of the Virginia State Capitol by Thomas Jefferson, based on the Maison Carrée. Right: At Nîmes, Jefferson ordered a wooden copy of a bronze askos (a wine or oil vessel) found among the ruins. When he returned to Monticello, the copy was reproduced in silver. The inscription on the lid reads: "Copy from a model taken in 1787 by Th. Jefferson from a Roman Ewer in the Cabinet of Antiquities at Nismes."

To Madame de Tessé

Here I am, Madam, gazing whole hours at the Maison quarrée, like a lover at his mistress. The stocking-weavers and silk spinners around it consider me as an hypochondriac Englishman, about to write with a pistol the last chapter of his history. This is the second time I have been in love since I left Paris. The first was with a Diana at the Chateau de Laye Epinaye in the Beaujolois, a delicious morsel of sculpture, by Michael Angelo Slodtz. This, you will say, was in rule, to fall in love with a fine woman: but, with a house! It is out of all precedent! No, madam, it is not without a precedent in my own history. While at Paris, I was violently smitten with the hotel de Salm, and used to go to the Thuileries almost daily to look at it. The loueuse des chaises, inattentive to my passion, never had the complaisance to place a chair there; so that, sitting on the parapet, and twisting my neck round to see the object of my admiration, I generally left it with a torticollis. From Lyons to Nismes I have been nourished with the remains of Roman grandeur. They have always brought you to my mind, because I know your affection for whatever is Roman and noble. At Vienne I thought of you. But I am glad you were not there; for you would have seen me more angry than I hope you will ever see me. The Pretorian palace, as it is called, comparable for it's fine proportions to the Maison quarrée, totally defaced by the Barbarians who have converted it to it's present purpose; it's beautiful, fluted, Corinthian columns cut out in part to make space for Gothic windows, and hewed down in the residue to the plane of the building. At Orange too I thought of you. I was sure you had seen with rapture the sublime triumphal arch at the entrance into the city. I went

Left: The Maison Carrée, the arena, and the Tour Magne in Nîmes by Hubert Robert, 1787. Above: Portrait of Madame de Tessé who was the aunt of the Marquis de Lafayette, a friend of Jefferson's who arranged their introduction in Paris. She was only a few years older than Jefferson when they met.

This is the second time I have been in love since I left Paris.

then to the Arenas. Would you believe Madam, that in [this 18th. centur]y, in France, und[er the reign of Louis XVI, they] are [at this mo]ment pulling down the circular wall of this superb remain [to pave a ro]ad? And that too from a hill which is itself an entire mass of stone just as fit, and more accessible. A former Intendant, a Monsr. de Baville has rendered his memory dear to travellers and amateurs by the pains he took to preserve and to restore these monuments of antiquity. The present one (I do not know who he is) is demolishing the object to make a good road to it. I thought of you again, and I was then in great good humour, at the Pont du Gard, a sublime antiquity, and [well] preserved. But most of all here, where Roman taste, genius, and magnificence excite ideas analogous to yours at every step, I could no longer oppose the inclination to avail myself of your permission to write to you, a permission given with too much complaisance by you, taken advantage of with too much indiscretion by me. Madame de Tott too did me the same honour. But she being only the descendant of some of those puny heroes who boiled their own kettles before the walls of Troy, I shall write to her from a Graecian, rather than a Roman canton; when I shall find myself for example among her Phocean relations at Marseilles. Loving, as you do Madam, the precious remains of antiquity, loving architecture, gardening, a warm sun, and a clear sky, I wonder you have never thought of moving Chaville to Nismes. This is not so impracticable as you may think. The next time a Surintendant des batiments du roi, after the example of M. Colbert, sends persons to Nismes to move the Maison [Car]rée to Paris, that they may not come empty-handed, desire them to bring Chaville with them to replace it. A propos of Paris. I have now been three weeks from there without knowing any thing of what has past. I suppose I shall meet it all [at Aix, where] I have directed my letters to be lodged poste restante. My journey has given me leisure to reflect on this Assemblée des Notables.

Under a good and young king as the present, I think good may be m[ade of it.] I would have the deputies then by all means so conduct themselves as [to encourage] him to repeat the calls of this assembly. Their first step should be to get th[emselves] divided into two chambers, instead of seven, the Noblesse and the commons separately. The 2d. to persuade the king, instead of chusing the deputies of the commons himself, to summon those chosen by the people for the Provincial administrations. The 3d. as the Noblesse is too numerous to be all admitted into the assemblée, to obtain permission for that body to chuse it's own deputies. The rest would follow. Two houses so elected would contain a mass of wisdom which would make the people happy, and the king great; would place him in history where no other act can possibly place him. This is my plan Madam; but I wish to know yours, which I am sure is better.

[From a correspondent at N]ismes you will not expect news. Were I [to attempt to give you news, I shoul]d tell you stories a thousand years old. [I should detail to you the intrigue]s of the courts of the Caesars, how they [affect us here, the oppressions of their] Praetors, Praefects &c. I am immersed [in antiquities from morning to night]. For me the city of Rome is actually [existing in all the splendor of it's] empire. I am filled with alarms for [the event of the irruptions dayly m]aking on us by the Goths, Ostrogoths, [Visigoths and Vandals, lest they shoul]d reconquer us to our original bar[barism. If I am sometimes ind]uced to look forward to the eighteenth [century, it is only when recalled] to it by the recollection of your goodness [and friendship, and by those sentiments of] sincere esteem and respect with which [I have the honor to be, Madam, your] most obedient & most humble servant,

Th: Jefferson

Above: The Interior of the Temple of Diana at Nîmes painted by Hubert Robert
Left: The Temple of Diana today

FROM WILLIAM SHORT

Paris March 22. 1787

My Dear Sir

Yours of the 15th. from Lyons arrived here on sunday last, and gave great pleasure to all your friends, to me a double portion because it shewed you were pleased with your journey and because it furnished me details on the country you passed through of which I was very desirous to be informed. I hope you will be so good as to continue them. Should I ever be able to make the same trip, they will be to me an useful guide. Should I not, they will be pleasing and useful information. The objects you propose to your attention are precisely those which, in my mind are the most worthy of it. As to manufactures they can be little useful to an American and for cabinets of curiosities he who has seen one complete one, has nothing left to see of the kind since he can have no farther curiosity on the subject.

...I have complyed with the other directions of your letter also, in presenting your compliments to your friends and more particularly to Mdes. de Tessé and de Tott. They both expressed the greatest satisfaction at hearing from you, and particularly at seeing that they were remembered by you. Their expressions were wound up to fortissimo, reducing them to forte, which I take to be the true tone of their friendship, and I think you may rely on the sincerity of all they said. ...Petit tells me that agreeably to your letter he waited on Miss Jefferson, and that she was and is perfectly well. I communicate this circumstance because I am sure of the pleasure it will give you.

Since your departure I have passed my time alternately two or three days at a time here and at St. Germains: yet in such a manner as to neglect nothing. It has been three days since I have returned from thence and do not purpose going there again before monday next. In the interim I hope to have the pleasure of hearing from you. Be persuaded my dear Sir, of the pleasure it will give Your sincerest friend & servant,

W Short

ABOVE: TEMPLE OF DIANA
RIGHT: JARDIN DE LA FONTAINE

The remains of antiquity . . . are more in number, & less injured by time, than I expected, and have been to me a great treat. Those at Nismes, both in dignity, & preservation, stand first.

THOMAS JEFFERSON, LETTER TO WILLIAM SHORT FROM AIX, MARCH 29, 1787

LEFT: ROMAN AMPHITHEATER IN NÎMES

Arles

On his way to Aix-en-Provence for the healing baths, Jefferson stopped in Arles. Built in the first century BC, the theater, which now stands in a walled garden, consists of two remaining marble columns, and some seating. The amphitheater, built later than the one in Nîmes, could seat twenty-six thousand people. Jefferson noted that "more than 1,000 people were still living within the arena." Many of the decorated sarcophagi that once lined the tree-shaded avenue called les Alyscamps, leading to the ruins of the Church of St. Honoratus, have disappeared. Today only a few remain in what was once one of the most famous burial grounds in the Western World. The church of St. Trophime, renowned for its doorway with Romanesque figures, its belfry, and its cloister, stands just off the Place de la République, near the Egyptian Obelisk moved in 1676 from a Roman circus across the Rhône. The Baths of Constantine date from the fourth century and are the only remains of Emperor Constantine's Palace.

Left: Cloister of St. Trophime, Arles

In the suburbs of Arles

MARCH 24. FROM NISMES TO ARLES....At an antient church in the suburbs of Arles are perhaps some hundreds of antient stone coffins along the road side. The ground is thence called les champs elysées. In a vault in the church are some preciously wrought, and in a back yard are many antient statues, inscriptions &c. Within the town are a part of two Corinthian columns, and of the pediment with which they were crowned, very rich, having belonged to the antient Capitol of the place. But the principal monument here is an Amphitheatre, the external portico of which is tolerably compleat....The ground floor is supported on innumerable vaults. The first story, externally, has a tall pedestal, like a pilaster, between every two arches: the upper story a column, the base of which would indicate it Corinthian. Every column is truncated as low as the impost of the arch, but the arches are all entire. The whole of the upper entablature is gone, and of the Attic, if there was one. Not a single seat of the internal is visible. The whole of the inside, and nearly the whole of the outside is masked by buildings. It is supposed there are 1000. inhabitants within the Amphitheatre. The walls are more entire and firm than those of the Amphitheatre at Nismes. I suspect it's plan and distribution to have been very different from that.

THOMAS JEFFERSON,
Notes of a Tour into the Southern Parts of France, &c.

RIGHT: ROMAN THEATER, ARLES

Above: Les Alyscamps
Left: Amphitheater
Right: Constantine's baths

Tarascon

Jefferson's next stop was in Tarascon, named for the mythical monster Tarasque. The Tarascon Castle, completed by "Good" King René in the fifteenth century, overhangs the Rhône. From its ramparts is an excellent view of Tarascon, Beaucaire, the Rhône valley, the Alpille mountains, and Arles.

Right: The castle at Tarascon

Saint-Rémy-de-Provence

Saint-Rémy was of interest to Jefferson for two reasons: its fame as a center for fruit and vegetable cultivation and its "Antiquities." Jefferson owned a 1777 print of these "fine ruins," consisting of a triumphal arch and a mausoleum of the ancient city of Glanum.

Archaeological excavations in this century have revealed the ancient Roman town of Glanum, which was built upon the remains of a Greek town founded in the second century BC.

Left: Ruins at Glanum

Far Left: Print of the "Vue de deux Monuments Antiques près de St.-Rémy-en-Provence, 1777," at Glanum, owned by Jefferson. Left: the Mausoleum at Glanum Above: the arch at Glanum.

An olive tree... lasts forever

St. Remis. From Terrasson to St. Remis is a plain of a league or two wide, bordered by broken hills of massive rock. It is grey and stony, mostly in olives. Some almonds, mulberries, willows, vines, corn and lucerne. Many sheep. No forest, nor inclosures.

...An olive tree must be 20 years old before it has paid it's own expences. It lasts for ever. In 1765. it was so cold that the Rhone was frozen over at Arles for 2. months. In 1767. there was a cold spell of a week which killed all the olive trees. From being fine weather in one hour there was ice hard enough to bear a horse. It killed people on the road.

Thomas Jefferson,
Notes of a Tour into the Southern Parts of France, &c.

PROVENCE

Aix-en-Provence

Jefferson arrived in Aix to treat his injured wrist at the baths. Founded by the Romans in 122 BC as Aquae Sextiae, Aix became a center of the arts and the Troubadour tradition in the fifteenth century, under "Good" King René. The famous street in the center of town, the Cours Mirabeau, is lined with plane trees and dotted with fountains. Jefferson admired the seventeenth- and eighteenth-century houses with their wrought-iron balconies supported by caryatids and atlantes.

The sixteenth-century wrought-iron clock tower in the Place de l'Hotel-de-Ville is next to the Town Hall. The Four Dolphins Fountain, built in 1667, sits in the lovely Place des Quatre Dauphins. The Vendôme Pavilion, also built in 1667, was constructed for the Cardinal de Vendôme in the form of an English house with a formal garden.

LEFT: HOTEL DE VILLE, AIX

From Martha Jefferson

March 25th, 1787

My dear Papa
Though the knowledge of your health gave me the greatest pleasure, yet I own I was not a little disappointed in not receiving a letter from you. However, I console myself with the thought of having one very soon, as you promised to write to me every week. Until now you have not kept your word the least in the world, but I hope you will make up for your silence by writing me a fine, long letter by the first opportunity.
...I expect Mr. Short every instant for my letter, therefore I must leave you. Adieu, my dear papa; be assured you are never a moment absent from my thoughts, and believe me to be, your most affectionate child,

M. Jefferson

From William Short

Paris March 26. 1787

Dear Sir

By my calculation I hoped to recieve your letter from Aix yesterday. Although it has not arrived I shall go into the country to-day, not foreseeing that the delay of one day in recieving it can be attended with any bad consequences. It will come to me at St. Germains in four and twenty hours and perhaps less after its arrival here if that should be before my return. I shall be four or five days absent and then come to Paris in order to do the honors of your house at Longchamp. I mentioned yesterday to Mde. de Tesse with whom I dined, what you had desired me, on this subject. She and Mde. de Tott were both much pleased with your attention. . . .

Wm. Short

Above and right: Garden in Aix

To William Short

Aix en Provence March. 27. 1787.

Dear Sir

I wrote to you on the 15th. from Lyons, and on my arrival here had the pleasure to find your favors of the 12th. and 14th. with the letters accompanying them....

I am now in the land of corn, wine, oil, and sunshine. What more can man ask of heaven? If I should happen to die at Paris I will beg of you to send me here, and have me exposed to the sun. I am sure it will bring me to life again. It is wonderful to me that every free being who possesses cent ecus de rente, does not remove to the Southward of the Loire. It is true that money will carry to Paris most of the good things of this canton. But it cannot carry thither it's sunshine, nor procure any equivalent for it. This city is one of the cleanest and neatest I have ever seen in any country. The streets are streight, from 20. to 100 feet wide, and as clean as a parlour floor. Where they are of width sufficient they have 1. 2. or 4. rows of elms from 100 to 150 years old, which make delicious walks. There are no portes-cocheres, so that the buildings shew themselves advantageously on the streets. It is in a valley just where it begins to open towards the mouth of the Rhone, forming in that direction a boundless plain which is an entire grove of olive trees, and is moreover in corn, lucerne, or vines, for the happiness of the olive tree is that it interferes with no superficial production. Probably it draws it's nourishment from parts out of the reach of any other plant. It takes well in every soil, but best where it is poorest, or where there is none. Comparing the Beaujolois with Provence, the former is of the richest soil, the latter richest in it's productions. But the climate of Beaujolois cannot be compared with this. I expect to find the situation of Marseilles still pleasanter: business will carry me thither soon, for a time at least. I can receive there daily the waters from this place, with no other loss

Above: Atlantes, Pavilion Vendôme

than that of their warmth, and this can easily be restored to them. I computed my journey on leaving Paris to be of 1000 leagues. I am now over one fourth of it. My calculation is that I shall conclude it in the earlier half of June. Letters may come to me here till the last day of April, about which time I shall be vibrating by this place Westwardly.—In the long chain of causes and effects, it is droll sometimes to seize two distant links and to present the one as the consequence of the other. Of this nature are these propositions. The want of dung prevents the progress of luxury in Aix. The poverty of the soil makes it's streets clean. These are legitimate consequences from the following chain. The preciousness of the soil prevents it's being employed in grass. Therefore no cattle, no dung. Hence the dung-gatherers (a numerous calling here) hunt it as eagerly in the streets as they would diamonds. Every one therefore can walk cleanly and commodiously. Hence few carriages. Hence few assemblies, routs, and other occasions for the display of dress.—I thank M. Pio for his anxieties on my account. My ostensible purpose of travelling without a servant was only to spare Espagnol the pain of being postponed to another, as I was quite determined to be master of my own secret, and therefore to take a servant who should not know me. At Fontainebleau I could not get one: but at Dijon I got a very excellent one who will probably go through the journey with me. Yet I must say, it is a sacrifice to opinion, and that without answering any one purpose worth a moment's consideration. They only serve to insulate me from the people among whom I am. Present me in the most friendly terms to M. Pio, M. Mazzei and other friends and believe me to be with the most sincere esteem your affectionate friend & servant,

Th: Jefferson

Above: Atlantes, Cours Mirabeau

To Martha Jefferson

Exercise and application produce order in our affairs, health of body, chearfulness of mind, and these make us precious to our friends. It is while we are young that the habit of industry is formed. If not then, it never is afterwards.

Aix en Provence

March. 28. 1787.

I was happy, my dear Patsy, to receive, on my arrival here, your letter informing me of your health and occupations. I have not written to you sooner because I have been almost constantly on the road. My journey hitherto has been a very pleasing one. It was undertaken with the hope that the mineral waters of this place might restore strength to my wrist. Other considerations also concurred. Instruction, amusement, and abstraction from business, of which I had too much at Paris. I am glad to learn that you are employed in things new and good in your music and drawing. You know what have been my fears for some time past; that you do not employ yourself so closely as I could wish. You have promised me a more assiduous attention, and I have great confidence in what you promise. It is your future happiness which interests me, and nothing can contribute more to it (moral rectitude always excepted) than the contracting a habit of industry and activity. Of all the cankers of human happiness, none corrodes it with so silent, yet so baneful a tooth, as indolence. Body and mind both unemployed, our being becomes a burthen, and every object about us loathsome, even the dearest. Idleness begets ennui, ennui the hypochondria, and that a diseased body. No laborious person was ever yet hysterical. Exercise and application produce order in our affairs, health of body, chearfulness of mind, and these make us precious to our friends. It is while we are young that the habit of industry

Right: Pavilion Vendôme, Aix

It is a part of the American character to consider nothing as desperate; to surmount every difficulty by resolution and contrivance.

is formed. If not then, it never is afterwards. The fortune of our lives therefore depends on employing well the short period of youth. If at any moment, my dear, you catch yourself in idleness, start from it as you would from the precipice of a gulph. You are not however to consider yourself as unemployed while taking exercise. That is necessary for your health, and health is the first of all objects. For this reason if you leave your dancing master for the summer, you must increase your other exercise. I do not like your saying that you are unable to read the antient print of your Livy, but with the aid of your master. We are always equal to what we undertake with resolution. A little degree of this will enable you to decypher your Livy. If you always lean on your master, you will never be able to proceed without him. It is a part of the American character to consider nothing as desperate; to surmount every difficulty by resolution and contrivance. In Europe there are shops for every want. It's inhabitants therefore have no idea that their wants can be furnished otherwise. Remote from all other aid, we are obliged to invent and to execute; to find means within ourselves, and not to lean on others. Consider therefore the conquering your Livy as an exercise in the habit of surmounting difficulties, a habit which will be necessary to you in the country where you are to live, and without which you will be thought a very helpless animal, and less esteemed. Music, drawing, books, invention and exercise will be so many resources to you against ennui. But there are others which to this object add that of utility. These are the needle, and domestic oeconomy. The latter you cannot learn here, but the former you may. In the country life of America there are many moments when a

> *In the country life of America there are many moments when a woman can have recourse to nothing but her needle for employment.*

woman can have recourse to nothing but her needle for employment. In a dull company and in dull weather for instance. It is ill manners to read; it is ill manners to leave them; no cardplaying there among genteel people; that is abandoned to blackguards. The needle is then a valuable resource. Besides without knowing to use it herself, how can the mistress of a family direct the works of her servants? You ask me to write you long letters. I will do it my dear, on condition you will read them from time to time, and practice what they will inculcate. Their precepts will be dictated by experience, by a perfect knowlege of the situation in which you will be placed, and by the fondest love for you. This it is which makes me wish to see you more qualified than common. My expectations from you are high: yet not higher than you may attain. Industry and resolution are all that are wanting. No body in this world can make me so happy, or so miserable as you. Retirement from public life will ere long become necessary for me. To your sister and yourself I look to render the evening of my life serene and contented. It's morning has been clouded by loss after loss till I have nothing left but you. I do not doubt either your affection or dispositions. But great exertions are necessary, and you have little time left to make them. Be industrious then, my dear child. Think nothing unsurmountable by resolution and application, and you will be all that I wish you to be. You ask me if it is my desire you should dine at the abbess's table? It is. Propose it as such to Madame de Traubenheim with my respectful compliments and thanks for her care of you. Continue to love me with all the warmth with which you are beloved by, my dear Patsy, yours affectionately,

Th: Jefferson

To William Short

Aix Mar. 29, 1787

Dear Sir

...In painting I have seen good things at Lyons only. In Architecture nothing any where except the remains of antiquity. These are more in number, and less injured by time than I expected, and have been to me a great treat. Those at Nismes, both in dignity and perservation, stand first. There is however at Arles an Amphitheatre as large as that of Nismes, the external walls of which from the top of the arches downwards is well preserved. Another circumstance contrary to my expectation is the change of language. I had thought the Provençale only a dialect of the French; on the contrary the French may rather be considered as a dialect of the Provençale. That is to say, the Latin is the original. Tuscan and Spanish are degeneracies in the first degree. Piedmontese (as I suppose) in the 2d. Provençale in the 3d. and Parisian French in the 4th. But the Provençale stands nearer to the Tuscan than it does to the French, and it is my Italian which enables me to understand the people here, more than my French. This language, in different shades occupies all the country South of the Loire. Formerly it took precedence of the French under the name of la langue Romans. The ballads of it's Troubadours were the delight of the several courts of Europe, and it is from thence that the novels of the English are called Romances. Every letter is pronounced, the articulation is distinct, no nasal sounds disfigure it, and on the whole it stands close to the Italian and Spanish in point of beauty. I think it a general misfortune that historical circumstances gave a final prevalence to the French instead of the Provençale language. It loses it's ground slowly, and will ultimately disappear because there are few books written in it, and because it is thought more polite to speak the language of the Capital. Yet those who learn that language here, pronounce it as the Italians do....

Be assured as to yourself that no person can more sincerely wish your prosperity and happiness, nor entertain warmer sentiments of esteem than Dear Sir your affectionate humble servant.

Left: Vue de la Principale Entrée de la Ville d'Aix in "Voyage Pittoresque de la France"

Above: Four Dolphins Fountain, 1667, Aix

GOLDEN

Marseilles

Between Aix-en-Provence and Nice, Jefferson spent two weeks visiting the seaports of Marseilles, Toulon, Hyéres, and Antibes. He originally planned to travel only as far as Nice, but he was not satisfied with what he had learned in Marseilles about processing rice, one of his many interests. He decided to travel to Italy for more research before returning to France for one of the main objectives of his trip, to see the Canal du Midi.

OVERLEAF: "ENTRANCE TO THE PORT OF MARSEILLES," BY JOSEPH VERNET, 1765

This is the work of women.

MAR. 29. MARSEILLES. The country is hilly, intersected by chains of hills and mountains of massive rock. The soil is reddish, stony and indifferent where best. Whenever there is any soil it is covered with olives. Among these are vines, corn, some lucerne, mulberry, some almonds and willow. Neither inclosures, nor forest. A very few sheep.

On the road I saw one of those little whirlwinds which we have in Virginia. Also some gullied hill-sides.

...The CAPER is a creeping plant. It is killed to the roots every winter. In the spring it puts out branches which creep to the distance of 3.f. from the center. The fruit forms on the stem as that extends itself, and must be gathered every day as it forms. This is the work of women.

...Marseilles is in an amphitheatre, at the mouth of the Vaune, surrounded by high mountains of naked rock...

THOMAS JEFFERSON,
Notes of a Tour into the
Southern Parts of France, &c.

FROM MARY JEFFERSON

[ca. 31 Mch. 1787)

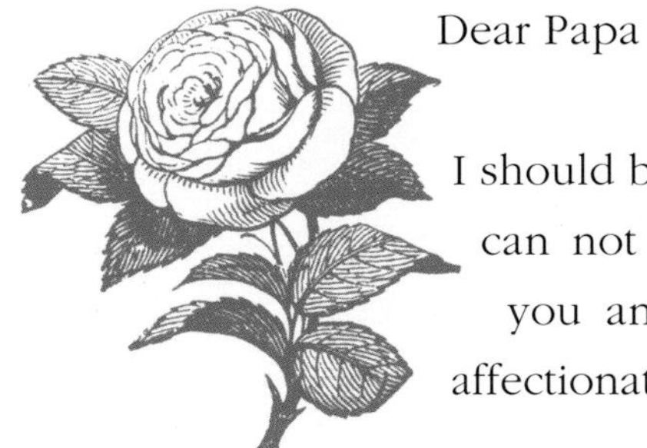

Dear Papa

I should be very happy to see you, but I can not go to France, and hope that you and sister Patsy are well. Your affectionate daughter. Adieu.

MARY JEFFERSON

To William Short

Toulon Apr. 7. 1787.

Dear Sir

I received yesterday at Marseilles your favor of Mar. 26. I was just then setting out for this place, and therefore deferred answering you till my arrival here.

...My wrist strengthens slowly: it is to time I look as the surest remedy, and that I believe will restore it at length. I set out tomorrow for Nice. The information received at Marseilles encourages me in my researches on the subject of rice, and that I shall meet with rice fields and the machines for cleaning it just beyond the Alps....Nothing can be ruder or more savage than the country I am in, as it must have come from the hands of nature; and nothing more rich and variegated in the productions with which art has covered it. Marseilles is a charming place. All life and activity, and a useful activity like London and Philadelphia. As I shall receive no more of your letters till I get back to Aix you will hear from me less often: probably not at all while beyond the Alps. When I get back to Nice I shall be able to calculate to a day my return to Aix, and of course the term after which it will be proper to send my letters to another stage. Remember me to enquiring friends, and be assured of the sincere esteem with which I am Dear Sir your affectionate friend & servant,

Th: Jefferson

Cannelle select
Cumin
Coriandre
Curry Bombay
Curry INDIAN

Nice

When Jefferson reached Nice, he was no longer in France but in a province of Sardinia, an historic resort ablaze with flowers and crowded with local produce markets. The Romans favored the Cimiez Hill district, and this is where Jefferson would have seen the almost-buried remains of Roman ruins. In Old Nice, he found many pastel Italianate buildings and narrow winding streets leading to the markets.

At the end of a three-week trip into Northern Italy (Piedmont area) to inspect the method of rice production, Jefferson returned to France by way of Menton, Monaco, and Nice. On May 1, he arrived exhausted in Menton after crossing the mountains between Italy and France by mule.

Left: Flower market, Old Nice

To Lafayette

Nice, April 11, 1787.

Your head, my dear friend, is full of Notable things; and being better employed, therefore, I do not expect letters from you. I am constantly roving about, to see what I have never seen before and shall never see again. In the great cities, I go to see what travellers think alone worthy of being seen; but I make a job of it, and generally gulp it all down in a day. On the other hand, I am never satiated with rambling through the fields and farms, examining the culture and cultivators, with a degree of curiosity which makes some take me to be a fool, and others to be much wiser than I am. I have been pleased to find among the people a less degree of physical misery than I had expected. They are generally well clothed, and have a plenty of food, not animal indeed, but vegetable, which is as wholesome. Perhaps they are over worked, the excess of the rent required by the landlord, obliging them to too many hours of labor, in order to produce that, and wherewith to feed and clothe themselves. . . . From the first olive fields of Pierrelate, to the orangeries of Hieres, has been continued rapture to me. I have often wished for you. I think you have not made this journey. It is a pleasure you have to come, and an improvement to be added to the many you have already made. It will be a great comfort to you to know, from your own inspection, the condition of all the provinces of your own country, and it will be interesting to them at some future day to be known to you. This is perhaps the only moment of your life in which you can acquire that knolege. And to do it most effectually you must be absolutely incognito, you must ferret the people out of their hovels as I have done, look into their kettles, eat their bread, loll on their beds under the pretence of resting yourself, but in fact to find if they are soft. You will feel a sublime pleasure in the course of this investigation, and a sublimer one hereafter when you shall be able to apply your knolege to the softening of their beds, or the throwing of a morsel of meat into the kettle of vegetables. You will not wonder at the subjects of my letter: they are the only ones which have been present in my mind for some time past, and the waters must always be what are the fountain from which they flow. According to this indeed I should have intermixed from beginning to end warm expressions of friendship to you; but according to the ideas of our country we do not permit ourselves to speak even truths when they may have the air of flattery. I content myself therefore with saying once and for all that I love you, your wife and children. Tell them so and Adieu. Your's affectionately,

Th: Jefferson

Left: Cimiez ruins

To William Short

Nice April 12. 1787.

Dear Sir
At Marseilles they told me I should encounter the ricefields of Piedmont soon after crossing the Alps. Here they tell me there are none nearer than Vercelli and Novarra, which is carrying me almost to Milan. I fear that this circumstance will occasion me a greater delay than I had calculated on. However I am embarked in the project and shall go through with it. Tomorrow I set out on my passage over the Alps, being to pursue it 93 miles to Coni on mules, as the snows are not yet enough melted to admit carriages to pass. I leave mine here therefore, proposing to return by water from Genoa. I think it will be three weeks before I get back to Nice.—I find this climate quite as superb as it has been represented. Hieres is the only place in France which may be compared with it. The climates are equal. In favor of this place are the circumstances of gay and dissipated society, a handsome city, good accomodations and some commerce. In favor of Hieres are environs of delicious and extensive plains, a society more contracted and therefore more capable of esteem, and the neighborhood of Toulon, Marseilles and other places to which excursions may be made. Placing Marseilles in comparison with Hieres, it has extensive society, a good theatre, freedom from military controul, and the most animated commerce. But it's winter climate far inferior.—I am now in the act of putting my baggage into portable form for my bat-mule; after praying you therefore to let my daughter know I am well and that I shall not be heard of again in three weeks I take my leave of you for that time with assurances of the sincere esteem with which I am Dear Sir your friend & servt.,

Th: Jefferson

The Southern Parts of France

297.—ALMOND.
AMYGDALUS COMMUNIS. Z. 135.
Pale red, white. 20 ft. Fl., 1½ in. Mar.—Ap.

…The Southern parts of France, but still more the passage thro' the Alps, enables one to form a scale of the tenderer plants, arranging them according to their several powers of resisting cold. Ascending three different mountains, Braus, Brois, and Tendé, they disappear one after another; and, descending on the other side, they shew themselves again one after another. This is their order, from the tenderest to the hardiest. Caper. orange. palm. aloe. olive. pomegranate. walnut. fig. almond. But this must be understood of the plant: for as to the fruit, the order is somewhat different. The caper, for example, is the tenderest plant; yet being so easily protected, it is the most certain in it's fruit. The almond, the hardiest plant, loses it's fruit the oftenest, on account of it's forwardness. The palm, hardier than the caper and the orange, never produces perfect fruit in these parts.…

THOMAS JEFFERSON,
Notes of a Tour into the Southern Parts of France, &c.

131.—COMMON CAPER.
CAPPARIS SPINOSA. G. 748.2.

LEFT: MUSÉE MASSÉNA, NICE

Menton, Monaco & Nice

Fragrant with abundant orange, lemon, and olive trees, Menton was bought by the Grimaldi family of Monaco in the fourteenth century and then returned to France, as was Nice, in 1860. The Old Town rises above the bay. Further up is the famous hill-town of Roquebrune, topped by the remains of a tenth-century Carolingian castle, the oldest in France.

Left: "Old town," Menton
Right: "Old town," Nice

MAY 1. VENTIMIGLIA. Menton. Monaco. Nice. At Bordighera between Ventimiglia and Menton are extensive plantations of palms on the hill as well as in the plain. They bring fruit but it does not ripen....From Menton to Monaco there is more good land, and extensive groves of oranges and lemons....

THOMAS JEFFERSON,
Notes of a Tour into the Southern Parts of France, &c.

ABOVE AND RIGHT: THE RIVIERA

TO MARTHA JEFFERSON

Marseilles May 5, 1787

And that you may be always doing good, my dear, is the ardent prayer of yours affectionately

My Dear Patsy

I got back to Aix the day before yesterday, and found there your letter of the 9th. of April, from which I presume you to be well tho' you do not say so. In order to exercise your geography I will give you a detail of my journey. You must therefore take your map and trace out the following places. Dijon, Lyons, Pont St. Esprit, Nismes, Arles, St. Remis, Aix, Marseilles, Toulon, Hieres, Frejus, Antibes, Nice, Col de Tende, Coni, Turin, Vercelli, Milan, Pavia, Tortona, Novi, Genoa, by sea to Albenga, by land to Monaco, Nice, Antibes, Frejus, Brignolles, Aix, and Marseille. The day after tomorrow I set out hence for Aix, Avignon, Pont du Gard, Nismes, Montpelier, Narbonne, along the Canal of Languedoc to Toulouse, Bourdeaux, Rochefort, Rochelle, Nantes, Lorient, Nantes, Tours, Orleans and Paris where I shall arrive about the middle of June, after having travelled something upwards of a thousand leagues. From Genoa to Aix was very fatiguing, the first two days having been at sea, and mortally sick, two more clambering the cliffs of the Appennine, sometimes on foot, sometimes on a mule according as the path was more or less difficult, and two others travelling thro' the night as well as day, without sleep. I am not yet rested, and shall therefore shortly give you rest by closing my letter, after mentioning that I have received a letter from your sister, which tho a year old, gave me great pleasure. I inclose it for your perusal, as I think it will be pleasing to you also. But take care of it, and return it to me when I shall get back to Paris, for trifling as it seems, it is precious to me. When I left Paris, I wrote to London to desire that your harpsichord might be sent during the months of April and May, so that I am in hopes it will arrive a little before I shall, and give me an opportunity of judging whether you have got the better of that want of industry which I had began to fear would be the rock on which you would split. Determine never to be idle. No person will have occasion to complain of the want of time, who never loses any. It is wonderful how much may be done, if we are always doing. And that you may be always doing good, my dear, is the ardent prayer of yours affectionately,

TH: JEFFERSON

RIGHT: LES BAUX

Left, above and right: One of the most spectacular sights in Provence, with sweeping views of the Camargue and the countryside, Les Baux sits high on a spur of the Alpilles. In the twelfth century, the Lords of Baux celebrated the troubadour tradition with their poetry and songs. In 1632, as a result of their doubtful loyalty, Louis XIII destroyed the castle and the ramparts. The ruins seem mysterious and haunting, even in the daylight.

Overleaf: View from Les Baux

Avignon & Vaucluse

In Avignon, Jefferson wanted to visit Laura's tomb in the Church of the Cordeliers and Petrarch's retreat in the Vaucluse. The Vaucluse spring is the source of the Sorgue River, which flows beneath Avignon. One of the most picturesque areas in Avignon is the rue des Teinturiers, where the Sorgue, now above ground, propelled the waterwheels of the dyers. The Palace of the Popes, Avignon's great fortress, is at the foot of the terraced gardens called Rocher des Domes. From the top of the park there is a superb view of St. Bénézet Bridge, which is the subject of "Sur le pont d'Avignon," a favorite song of childhood.

Left and right: Bridge at Avignon

Willows, mulberries, vines, corn and pasture...

MAY 8. ORGON. AVIGNON. VAUCLUSE. AVIGNON....from Orgon to Avignon is entirely a plain of rich dark loam, which is in willows, mulberries, vines, corn and pasture....In the valley of Vaucluse and on the hills impending over it are Olive trees....

THOMAS JEFFERSON,
Notes of a Tour into the Southern Parts of France, &c.

RIGHT: THE VERDANT FIELDS OF PROVENCE

...this fountain, a noble one of itself, and rendered forever famous by the songs of Petrarch...

THOMAS JEFFERSON

LEFT: VUE DE LA FONTAINE DE VAUCLUSE ET DES ENVIRONS, "VOYAGE PITTORESQUE DE LA FRANCE"
ABOVE: FONTAINE DE VAUCLUSE TODAY

During the reign of Louis XIV, Montpellier was the capital of Lower Languedoc. The Old Town has many lovely seventeenth-century mansions showing Italian influences. The Peyrou Promenade, with its rows of plane trees, offers fine views of the mountains. In Montpellier, Jefferson attended the theater, perhaps in the Place de la Comedie, decorated at one end with the Three Graces, an eighteenth-century fountain. From Montpellier Jefferson traveled to Sète on the Mediterranean, sailing from Sète through the Etang de Thau to Agde. There he decided to remove the wheels of his carriage and place it on a private "bark" for the nine-day trip to Toulouse.

LEFT: FOUNTAIN OF THE THREE GRACES
RIGHT: DOOR KNOCKER

Béziers

Béziers was colonized by Julius Caesar's legionaries shortly after his conquest of Gaul. By the Middle Ages, the town was a thriving way station on the "silk route," where spices and other luxury imports from the East made their way to France. In Béziers, Jefferson probably walked to the thirteenth-century Cathedral of St. Nazaire, atop a stony bluff, which offered a panoramic view of the countryside across the river Orb. A commemorative statue to Pierre-Paul Riquet, the genius behind the construction of the Canal du Midi, stands in the town's most beautiful thoroughfare. The Allées Paul-Riquet leads to the "Plateau des Poètes," one of the loveliest parks in the Languedoc.

Left: Cathedral of St. Nazaire, Béziers

A SHORT HISTORY OF THE CANAL DU MIDI

A waterway linking the Atlantic and the Mediterranean had been discussed since Roman times. Suggestions for its construction were made in the eighth century, under Charlemagne. Francis I discussed the project with Leonardo da Vinci in 1516. Charles IX and Henry IV considered it in the sixteenth century, as well as Louis XIII in 1633. It was not until the relatively stable reign of Louis XIV, however, that work was actually begun on what, thanks to the lifelong and untiring efforts of Pierre Paul Riquet, became the 'Canal Royal du Languedoc', known today as the Canal du Midi.

Begun in 1667, the official opening of the 'Canal Royal' occurred on May 15, 1681, celebrated by a grand procession of vessels carrying freight and dignitaries from Toulouse to l'Etang du Thau, after a voyage of ten days. Unfortunately, Riquet, whose dreams and accomplishment were "the greatest feat of engineering since that of the Romans," had died eight months earlier, just before the completion of the last section of the Canal, from Agde to l'Etang du Thau.

When, in 1856, the Garonne River was canalized to link Bordeaux with Toulouse, the completed waterway, "from sea to sea," providing safe and relatively rapid trans-

port from the Atlantic to the Mediterranean, the economy of the Languedoc was increased to new heights. Today, three centuries later, the canal continues to benefit both trade and tourism.

In order to limit the costs of terracing, Riquet followed the natural contours of the land whenever possible. As a result, unlike many canals, the Canal du Midi meanders through a variety of landscapes, encountering vineyards, olive groves, the Lauragais area (the traditional granary of the South for centuries), towns and cities, both ancient and modern. Among these are Toulouse, in whose cathedral of St. Etienne Riquet is buried; Castelnaudary, whose farsighted citizens paid Riquet to divert his canal to their town; Carcassonne, whose citizens refused to pay for a diversion, with the result that the canal bypasses the town; Argens-Minervoie, "the most beautiful village on the Canal du Midi"; Capestang, the site of the world's largest vineyard, where the *gros-rouge*, the everyday table wines of France, are produced; Fonserannes, location of the seven-lock "stairway," unique in the French canal system; Béziers, the birthplace of Riquet; and finally l'Etang du Thau, on the edge of the Camargue, where the Canal du Midi joins the Mediterranean.

Roy & Alma Moore

Left: Pont Riquet, Canal du Midi, Seventeenth Century

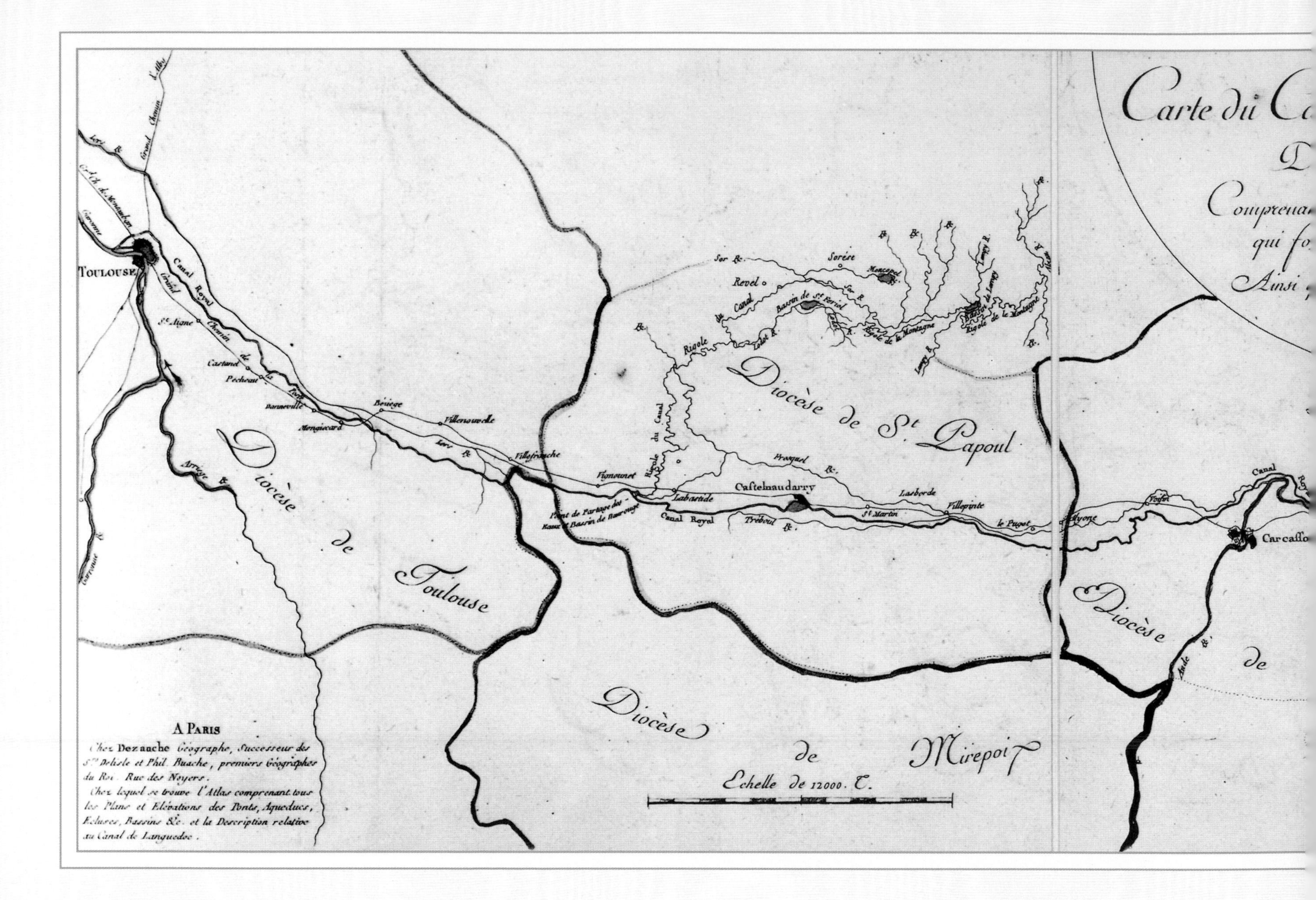
Carte du Ca
Compren
qui fo
Ainsi
TOULOUSE
Canal Royal
Castelnaudarry
Villefranche
Revel
Sorèse
Villenouvelle
Baziège
Montgiscard
St Martin
Villepinte
Labastide
le Puget
Lasborde
Canal Royal
Rigole de la Montagne
Bassin de St Ferriol
Rigole du Canal
Dioceèse de Toulouse
Diocèse de St Papoul
Diocèse de Mirepoix
Diocèse de
Carcasso
Echelle de 12000. T.
A PARIS
Chez Dezauche Géographe, Successeur des
Srs Delisle et Phil. Buache, premiers Géographes
du Roi. Rue des Noyers.
Chez lequel se trouve l'Atlas comprenant tous
les Plans et Elévations des Ponts, Aqueducs,
Ecluses, Bassins &c. et la Description relative
au Canal de Languedoc.

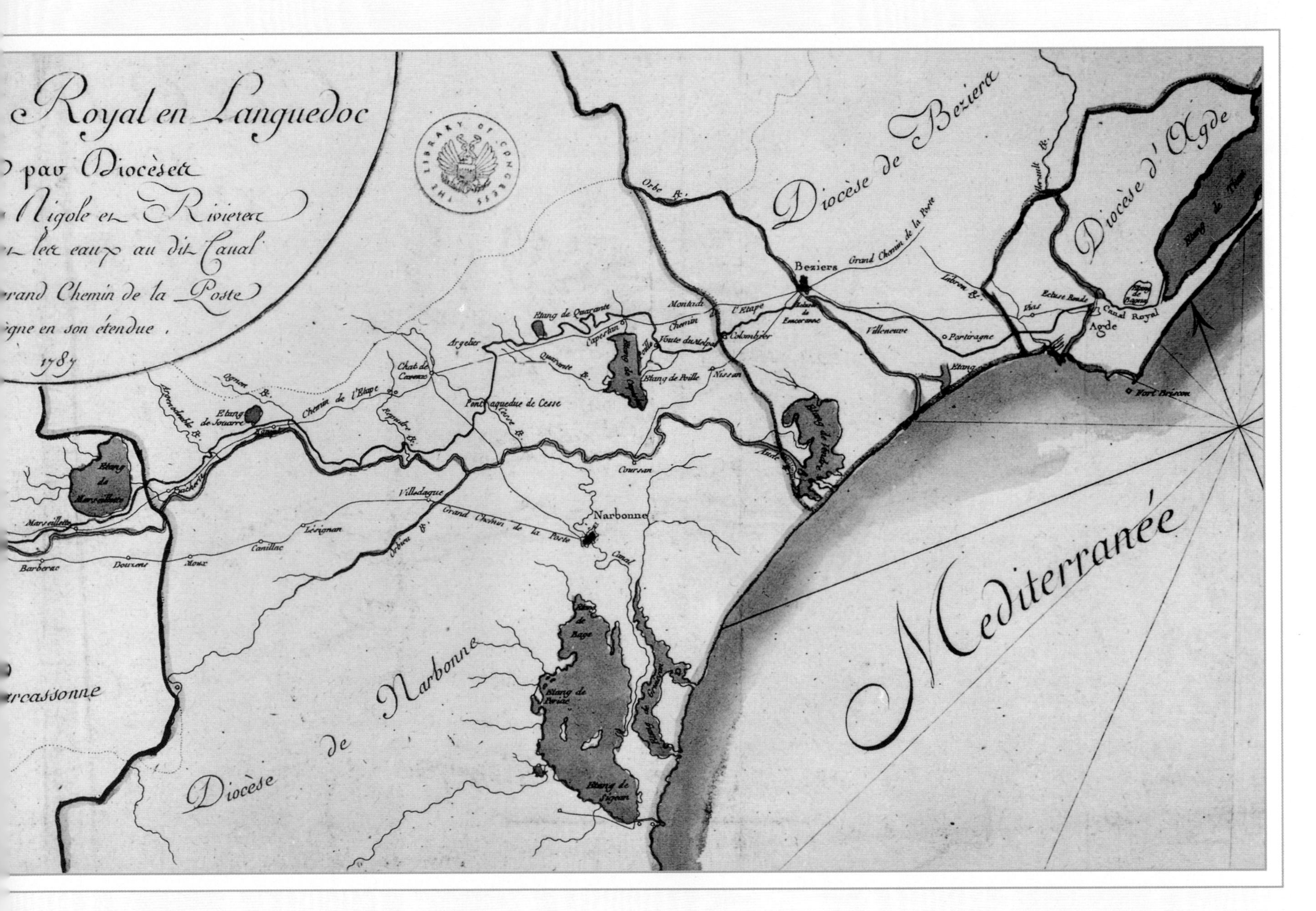

THOMAS JEFFERSON SENT THIS MAP TO GEORGE WASHINGTON ALONG WITH HIS LETTER OF MAY 2, 1788. THE MAP WAS PRINTED IN PARIS BY DEZAUCHE IN 1787.

The Canal of Languedoc

[The Canal of Languedoc along which I now travel is 6. toises wide at bottom, and 10 toises at the surface of the water, which is 1. toise deep. The barks which navigate it are 70. and 80. feet long, and 17. or 18. f. wide. They are drawn by one horse, and worked by 2. hands, one of which is generally a woman. The locks are mostly kept by women, but the necessary operations are much too laborious for them.] The encroachments by the men on the offices proper for the women is a great derangement in the order of things. Men are shoemakers, tailors, upholsterers, staymakers, mantua makers, cooks, door-keepers, housekeepers, housecleaners, bedmakers. They coëffe the ladies, and bring them to bed: the women therefore, to live are obliged to undertake the offices which they abandon. They become porters, carters, reapers, wood cutters, sailors, lock keepers, smiters on the anvil, cultivators of the earth &c. Can we wonder if such of them as have a little beauty prefer easier courses to get their livelihood, as long as that beauty lasts? Ladies who employ men in the offices which should be reserved for their sex, are they not bawds in effect? For every man whom they thus employ, some girl, whose place he has taken, is driven to whoredom.

THOMAS JEFFERSON,
Notes of a Tour into the Southern Parts of France, &c.

Malpas Tunnel, May 16, 1787.

Leaving Béziers, Jefferson's "bark" passed through the "eight-step" staircase locks at Fonserannes, crossed the Orb River, and proceeded to the Malpas Tunnel. Riquet's tunnel bores through the Ensérune hill and was constructed by hand in only six days.

Ensérune

From the top of Ensérune, a sixth-century fortified hill town, is a view of the ancient Montady Pool, once a large lagoon and now farmland. Radiating drainage ditches, originally built to empty the lagoon, converge upon the circle in such a way as to create the illusion that the entire area slopes to the center.

Carcassonne

Jefferson could see this medieval fortress from the Canal du Midi. The Romans fortified the old town, "La Cité," of Carcassonne in the first century BC. Double ramparts protected the fortress even from a five-year siege by Charlemagne in the ninth century. The fortress and town were later abandoned and fell into ruins during the Albigensian Crusade. In 1854, the architect Violet-le-Duc began restoration of the city, the ramparts, and the towers. Carcassonne's reconstruction was the first in the world to be carried out on such a large scale. A sixteenth-century bridge provides an entrance to the city.

Left: Medieval fortress of Carcassonne
Overleaf: Carcassonne at dusk

MAY 17. MARSEILLETTE. CARCASSONNE. [From Saumal to Carcassonne we have always the river Aube close on our left. This river runs in the valley between the Cevennes and Pyrenees, serving as the common receptacle for both their waters. It is from 50. to 150. yards wide, always rapid, rocky, and insusceptible of navigation. The canal passes in the side of the hills made by that river, overlooks the river itself, and it's plains, and has it's prospect ultimately terminated, on one side by mountains of rock overtopped by the Pyrenees, on the other by small mountains, sometimes of rock, sometimes of soil overtopped by the Cevennes. Marseillette is on a ridge which separates the river Aube from the etang de Marseillette. The canal, in it's approach to this village, passes the ridge, and rides along the front overlooking the etang and the plains on it's border; and having passed the village recrosses the ridge and resumes it's general ground in front of the Aube.] The growth is corn, St. foin, pasture, vines, mulberries, willows, and olives.

MAY 18. CARCASSONNE. CASTELNAUDARI....I observe them fishing in the canal with a skimming net of about 15. feet diameter, with which they tell me they catch carp. Flax in blossom. Neither strawberries nor peas yet at Carcassonne. The Windsor bean just come to table....

THOMAS JEFFERSON,
Notes of a Tour into the Southern Parts of France, &c.

RIGHT: ENTRANCE BRIDGE TO CARCASSONNE

Castelnaudary

At Castelnaudary, Jefferson's barge and carriage entered the lagoon, or "Grand Bassin," which feeds the five locks of Saint-Roch. His interest in mechanical devices would have led him to inspect the seventeenth-century windmill at the top of Pech hill. In the town, sixteenth- and seventeenth-century houses are found in the old quarter.

Left: Canal along Castelnaudary
Right: Windmill at Castelnaudary

Indian corn

MAY 19. CASTELNAUDARI....Round about Castelnaudari the country is hilly, as it has been constantly from Beziers. It is very rich. Where it is plain, or nearly plain, the soil is black: in general however it is hilly and reddish, and in corn. They cultivate a great deal of Indian corn here, which they call Millet. It is planted, but not yet up.

THOMAS JEFFERSON,
Notes of a Tour into the
Southern Parts of France, &c.

RIGHT: LAGOON AT CASTELNAUDARY

The passage of the eight locks at Bezieres, that is from the opening of the 1st. to the last gate took 1. Hour 33'....The canal yields an abundance of carp and eel. I see also small fish resembling our perch and chub. Some plants of white clover, and some of yellow on the banks of the canal near Capestan; Santolina also and a great deal of yellow Iris....The extensive and numerous fields of St. foin, in general bloom, are beautiful.

THOMAS JEFFERSON,
Notes of a Tour into the Southern Parts of France, &c.

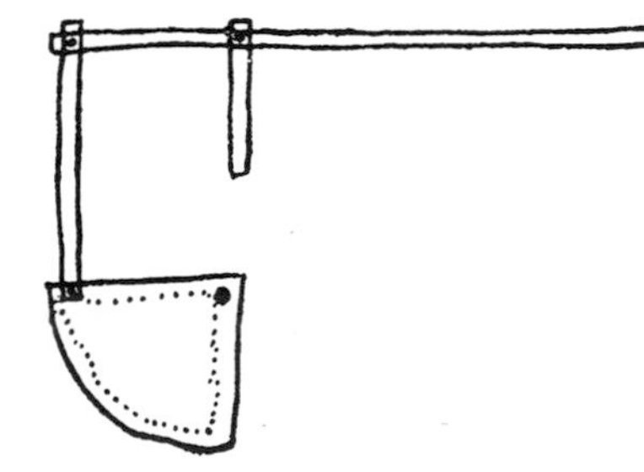

TOP AND RIGHT: LOCKS AT THE CANAL DU MIDI
ABOVE: A DRAWING OF A LOCK LEVER FROM THOMAS JEFFERSON'S NOTEBOOKS
FAR RIGHT: LOCKKEEPER'S HOUSE

E FONFILE.
NCES:
DE L'ÉCLUSE
DE St-MARTIN.
1242 MÈTRES

TO MARTHA JEFFERSON

May 21. 1787.

I write to you, my dear Patsy, from the Canal of Languedoc, on which I am at present sailing, as I have been for a week past, cloudless skies above, limpid waters below, and on each hand a row of nightingales in full chorus. This delightful bird had given me a rich treat before at the fountain of Vaucluse. After visiting the tomb of Laura at Avignon, I went to see this fountain, a noble one of itself, and rendered for ever famous by the songs of Petrarch who lived near it. I arrived there somewhat fatigued, and sat down by the fountain to repose myself. It gushes, of the size of a river, from a secluded valley of the mountain, the ruins of Petrarch's chateau being perched on a rock 200 feet perpendicular above. To add to the enchantment of the scene, every tree and bush was filled with nightingales in full song. I think you told me you had not yet noticed this bird. As you have trees in the garden of the convent, there must be nightingales in them, and this is the season of their song. Endeavor, my dear, to make yourself acquainted with the music of this bird, that when you return to your own country you may be able to estimate it's merit in comparison with that of the mocking bird. The latter has the advantage of singing thro' a great part of the year, whereas the nightingale sings but 5. or 6. weeks in the spring, and a still shorter term and with a more feeble voice in the fall. I expect to be at Paris about the middle of next month. By that time we may begin to expect our dear Polly. It will be a circumstance of inexpressible comfort to me to have you both with me once more. The object most interesting to me for the residue of my life, will be to see you both developing daily those principles of virtue and goodness which will make you valuable to others and happy in yourselves, and acquiring those talents and that degree of science which will guard you at all times against ennui, the most dangerous poison of life. A mind always employed is always happy. This is the true secret, the grand recipe for felicity. The idle are the only wretched. In a world which furnishes so many emploiments which are useful, and so many which are amusing, it is our own fault if we ever know what ennui is, or if we are ever driven to the miserable resource of gaming, which corrupts our dispositions, and teaches us a habit of hostility against all mankind.—We are now entering the port of Toulouse, where I quit my bark; and of course must conclude my letter. Be good and be industrious, and you will be what I shall most love in this world. Adieu my child. Yours affectionately,

Th: Jefferson

RIGHT: SIGHTS ALONG THE CANAL

A mind always
employed is always happy.
This is the true secret,
the grand recipe
for felicity.

To William Short

On the Canal of Languedoc,
approaching Toulouse. May 21. 1787.

...I have passed through the Canal from it's entrance into the mediterranean at Cette to this place, and shall be immediately at Toulouse, in the whole 200 American miles, by water; having employed in examining all it's details nine days, one of which was spent in making a tour of 40 miles on horseback, among the Montagnes noires, to see the manner in which water has been collected to supply the canal; the other eight on the canal itself. I dismounted my carriage from it's wheels, placed it on the deck of a light bark, and was thus towed on the canal instead of the post road. That I might be perfectly master of all the delays necessary, I hired a bark to myself by the day, and have made from 20. to 35 miles a day, according to circumstances, always sleeping ashore. Of all the methods of travelling I have ever tried this is the pleasantest. I walk the greater part of the way along the banks of the canal, level, and lined with a double row of trees which furnish shade. When fatigued I take seat in my carriage where, as much at ease as if in my study, I read, write, or observe. My carriage being of glass all round, admits a full view of all the varying scenes thro' which I am shifted, olives, figs, mulberries, vines, corn and pasture, villages and farms. I have had some days of superb weather, enjoying two parts of the Indian's wish, cloudless skies and limpid waters: I have had another luxury which he could not wish, since we have driven him from the country of Mockingbirds, a double row of nightingales along the banks of the canal, in full song. This delicious bird gave me another rich treat at Vaucluse. Arriving there a little fatigued I sat down to repose myself at the fountain . . .and every tree and bush filled with nightingales in full chorus. I find Mazzei's observation just that their song is more varied, their tone fuller and stronger here than on the banks of the Seine. It explains to me another circumstance, why there never was a poet North of the Alps, and why there never will be one. A poet is as much the creature of climate as an orange or palm tree. What a bird the nightingale would be in the climates of America! We must colonize him thither. You should not think of returning to America without taking the tour which I have taken ...

Th: Jefferson

Left: The canal at sunset

Toulouse

Jefferson's final stop on the Canal du Midi was the rosy brick city of Toulouse, which boasted magnificent houses of the twelfth to the eighteenth centuries and the Basilica of St. Sernin. At the Ponts-Jumeaux, a sculpted relief by François Lucas marks the meeting place for the Canal du Midi, with the present day Canal à la Garonne and the Canal Lateral. At Toulouse, Jefferson replaced the wheels on his carriage and left for Bordeaux and the Atlantic coast on his return to Paris.

Left: Antique column
Right: Architectural detail in Toulouse

P

Fields of yellow clover

MAY 21. BAZIEGE. TOULOUSE. The country continues hilly, but very rich. It is in mulberries, willows, some vines, corn, maize, pasture, beans, flax. A great number of chateaux and good houses in the neighborhood of the canal. The people partly in farm houses, partly in villages. I suspect that the farm houses are occupied by the farmer, while the labourers (who are mostly by the day) reside in the villages. Neither strawberries nor peas yet at Baziege or Toulouse. Near the latter are some feilds of yellow clover.

THOMAS JEFFERSON,
Notes of a Tour into the Southern Parts of France, &c.

LEFT: PONTS-JUMEAUX (WHERE THE CANAL DU MIDI MEETS CANAL A LA GARONNE AND CANAL LATERAL)

FROM MARTHA JEFFERSON

Paris, May 27th, 1787.

My Dear Papa
I was very glad to see by your letter that you were on your return, and I hope that I shall very soon have the pleasure of seeing you. My sister's letter gave me a great deal of happiness. I wish she would write to me; but as I shall enjoy her presence very soon, it will make up for a neglect that I own gives me the greatest pain. I still remember enough of geography to know where the places marked in your letter are. I intend to copy over my extracts and learn them by heart. . . .Pray how does your arm go? I am very well now. Adieu, my dear papa; as I do not know any news, I must finish in assuring you of the sincerest affection of your loving child,

M. JEFFERSON

Paris May 2. 1788.

Sir

I am honoured with your Excellency's letter by the last packet & thank you for the information it contained on the communication between the Cayahoga & Big beaver. I have ever considered the opening a canal between those two watercourses as the most important work in that line which the state of Virginia could undertake. it will infallibly turn thro the Patowmack all the commerce of Lake Erie & the country West of that, except what may pass down the Missisipi. and it is important that it be soon done, lest that commerce should in the mean time get established in another channel. having in the spring of the last year taken a journey through the Southern parts of France, & particularly examined the canal of Languedoc through it's whole course, I take the liberty of sending you the notes I made on the spot, as you may find in them something perhaps which may be turned to account some time or other in the prosecution of the Patowmac canal. being merely a copy from my travelling notes they are indigested & imperfect, but may still perhaps give hints capable of improvement in your mind.

The affairs of Europe are in such a state still that it is impossible to say what form they will take ultimately. France & Prussia, viewing the Emperor as their most dangerous & common enemy had heretofore seen their common safety as depending on a strict connection with

His Excellency General Washington

life first, & then hereditary. I was much an enemy to monarchy before I came to Europe. I am ten thousand times more so since I have seen what they are. there is scarcely an evil known in these countries which may not be traced to their king as it's source, nor a good which is not derived from the small fibres of republicanism existing among them. I can further say with safety there is not a crowned head in Europe whose talents or merit would entitle him to be elected a vestryman by the people of any parish in America. however I shall hope that before there is danger of this change taking place in the office of President, the good sense & free spirit of our countrymen will make the changes necessary to prevent it. under this hope I look forward to the general adoption of the new constitution with anxiety, as necessary for us under our present circumstances.

I have so much trespassed on your patience already by the length of this letter that I will add nothing further than those assurances of sincere esteem & attachment with which I have the honor to be

Your Excellency's most obedient

& most humble servant

Th: Jefferson

Original letter written by Thomas Jefferson from Paris to George Washington on May 2, 1788.

To George Washington

Paris May 2. 1788

Sir

I am honoured with your Excellency's letter by the last packet and thank you for the information it contained on the communication between the Cayahoga and Big beaver. I have ever considered the opening of a canal between these two great watercourses as the most important work in that line which the state of Virginia could undertake. It will infallibly turn thro the Patowmack all the commerce of Lake Erie and the country West of that, except what may pass down the Missisipi. And it is important that it be soon done, lest that commerce should in the mean time get established in another channel. Having in the spring of the last year taken a journey through the Southern parts of France, and particularly examined the canal of Languedoc through it's whole course, I take the liberty of sending you the notes I made on the spot, as you may find in them something perhaps which may be turned to account some time or other in the prosecution of the Patowmac canal. Being merely a copy from my travelling notes, they are indigested and imperfect, but may still perhaps give hints capable of improvement in your mind....

Th : Jefferson

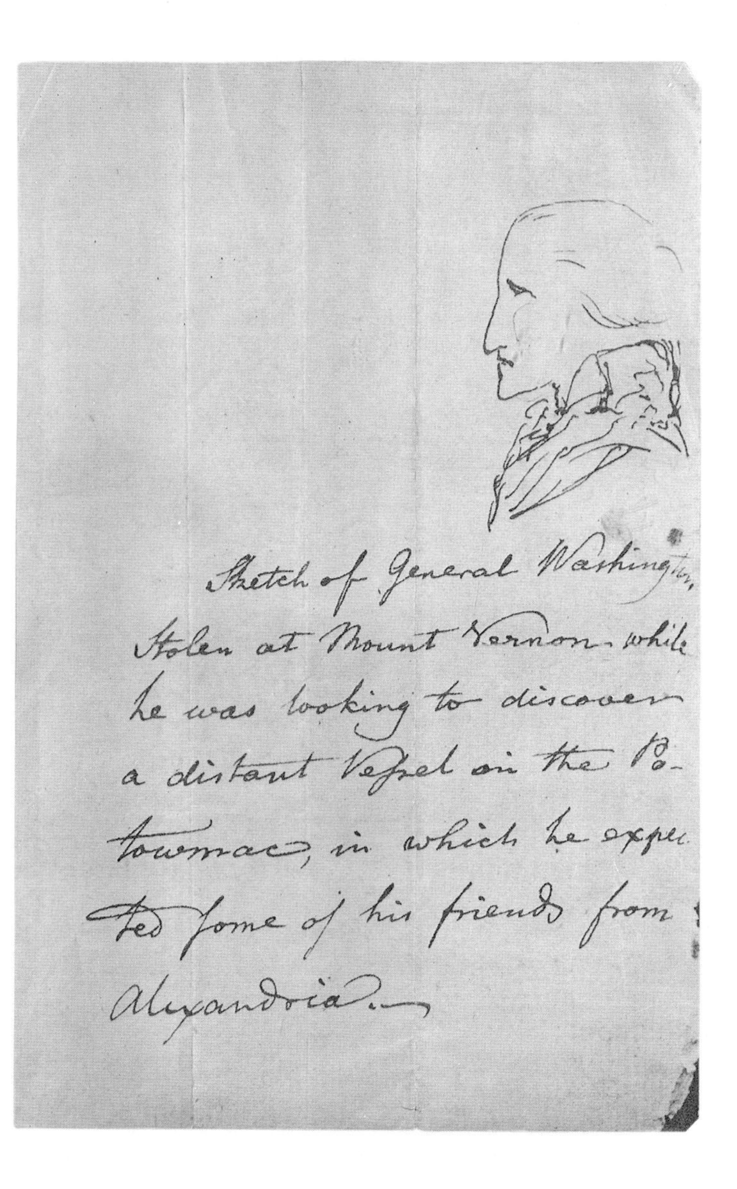

Sketch of George Washington by Benjamin Henry Latrobe

From a Letter to Thomas Jefferson from Madame de Tessé

30 March 1787

I have been projected into future ages, and have seen the youth of America reading with enthusiasm and admiration all that has been collected about your travels. When the wealth of her soil and the excellence of her government have elevated North America to the summit of greatness, when the southern continent has followed her example, when you have succored half the globe, then perhaps, people will search for the vestiges of Paris as they do today those of ancient Babylon, and the memoirs of Mr. Jefferson will guide travellers eagerly seeking antiquities of Rome and of France, which will then be as one.

Madame de Tessé

A Note on the Making of This Book

After five years as American minister to the court of France, Thomas Jefferson left Europe in 1789 for what he believed would be a short visit to America. He never returned. Washington asked him to serve as secretary of state and then, of course, he became our third American President. But he always felt that France was his second home, and to the end of his days remembered his three-month journey to the South of France.

Before he began his trip south he saw Hubert Robert's exhibition of paintings of Roman architecture and ruins (many of which are reproduced here.) Jefferson also admired Joseph Vernet's paintings of the French ports, including the one reproduced on pages 88-89.

This book tells the story of Jefferson's tour with those paintings, our photographs and letters written to and by Jefferson.

We followed his steps from Paris to Marseilles, from Nice to Toulouse, north to south, east to west. We hope you will decide to see it for yourself one day soon. For as Jefferson advised William Short, "you should not return to America without taking the tour I have just made." Short took his advice.

Acknowledgments

The idea for this book germinated on a barge drifting down the Canal du Midi many years ago. After that lovely week, we visited our dear friend Yvonne in her little house and garden in the hills above Menton. We talked of Roman ruins and lovers of Roman ruins, including Thomas Jefferson. We told Yvonne he had also spent nine days on the canal we had just left. This book grew out of that conversation.

We want to thank our editor, Linda Sunshine, for her vision and thoughtful approach to our book. We thank Mary Tiegreen, fellow Francophile and talented designer. Lucia Stanton's delightful introduction mirrors her fascinating insights into Thomas Jefferson's love of France, which she shared with us. Our appreciation, too, to Daniel P. Jordan, President, Thomas Jefferson Memorial Foundation, and Whitney T. Espich, Communications Officer, for her kindness in granting permission, including paintings from private collections and from Monticello. Thanks to Jennifer Tolpa of the Massachusetts Historical Society; Pamela Greiff, Boston Athenaeum, and Fred Bauman, Library of Congress, for their research and information.

Warm thanks to the Count and Countess de Fleurieu of the Château de Laye for their hospitality and permission to use the antique print from their personal collection on page 31. To Frances Bannett for her French translations and liaisons with France, and Avril and Olivier Lewis in St. Rémy and the Vaucluse. Finally, and importantly, to Princeton University Press for their permission to use the letters of Thomas Jefferson from "The Papers of Thomas Jefferson."

ROY AND ALMA MOORE

Thomas Jefferson's letters and all letters to him from his family and friends reprinted in this book are from "The Papers of Thomas Jefferson," edited by Julian P. Boyd. Copyright © 1955 by Princeton University Press. Used with permission.

Jacket Portrait: Painting of Thomas Jefferson by Mather Brown, 1786. Courtesy of Charles Francis Adams. Thomas Jefferson's handwriting from a letter to Eliza House Trist, February 23, 1787, from the Massachusetts Historical Society.

Page 6: Map of the South of France by Mary Tiegreen.

Page 9: Miniature of Maria Cosway by Richard Cosway from Huntington Library/Superstock.

Page 19: Jefferson's ivory notebooks, Monticello/Thomas Jefferson Memorial Foundation, Inc., Charlottesville, Virginia. Photograph by Edward Owen.

Page 24: Miniature of Martha Jefferson by Joseph Boze. Photograph by Will Brown. Diplomatic reception rooms, United States Department of State.

Page 31: Drawing of "Vue Du Château St. Denis-Espinay" from the private collection of the owners of the Château de Laye.

Page 39: Painting of the Triumphal Arch and Theater, Orange, by Hubert Robert (1733-1808). Photograph by Gérard Blot © RMN. Musée du Louvre.

Page 42: Painting of the Pont du Gard by Hubert Robert (1733-1808). Photograph by Gérard Blot © RMN. Musée du Louvre.

Page 46: Sketch of the front elevation of the Virginia State Capitol by Thomas Jefferson from the Massachusetts Historical Society, Boston.

Page 47: *Askos* belonging to Thomas Jefferson from Monticello/ Thomas Jefferson Memorial Foundation, Inc., Charlottesville, Virginia.

Page 48: Painting of the Maison Carrée by Hubert Robert (1733-1808). Photograph by Gérard Blot © RMN. Musée du Louvre.

Page 49: Portrait of Madame de Tessé, artist unknown. M. Paul de Larminat. Courtesy of François Schlumberger.

Page 53: Painting of the Interior of the Temple of Diana at Nîmes by Hubert Robert (1733-1808). Photograph by Gérard Blot © RMN. Musée du Louvre.

Page 69: Print of the "Vue de deux Monuments Antiques près de St. Rémy en Provence," 1777. Painting by C. Lamy, engraved for sale at Paris and St. Rémy. Monticello/Thomas Jefferson Memorial Foundation, Inc., Charlottesville, Virginia.

Page 84: Print of the "Vue de la Principale Entrée de la Ville d'Aix," engraving from a drawing by Meunieur, Plate No. 2, Départ. Des Bouches du Rhône. Reproduced from "Voyage Pittoresque de la France," compiled by Laborde, Guettard, and Béguillet, Paris, 1784-1802. The Boston Athenaeum.

Pages 88-89: Painting of "L'entrée du Port de Marseilles" (1765) by Joseph Vernet (1714-1789). Musée du Louvre. Photograph by R. G. Ojeda, P. Neri © RMN. Musée de Louvre.

Page 118: Print of "Vue de la Fountain de Vauclause et des Environs" from a drawing by Genillon, Plate No. 76, Provence. Reproduced from "Voyage Pittoresque de la France," compiled by Laborde, Guettard, and Béguillet, Paris, 1784-1802. The Boston Athenaeum.

Pages 128-129: Map of the Canal of Languedoc, printed in 1787, courtesy of the Library of Congress.

Page 156: Letter by Thomas Jefferson to George Washington, May 2, 1788. Courtesy of the Library of Congress.

Page 157: Sketch of George Washington by Benjamin Henry Latrobe, from the collection of the Maryland Historical Society, Baltimore, Maryland.

Endpapers: Map of the Canal du Midi from the archives of the Canal du Midi. Courtesy of Éditions Loubatières.

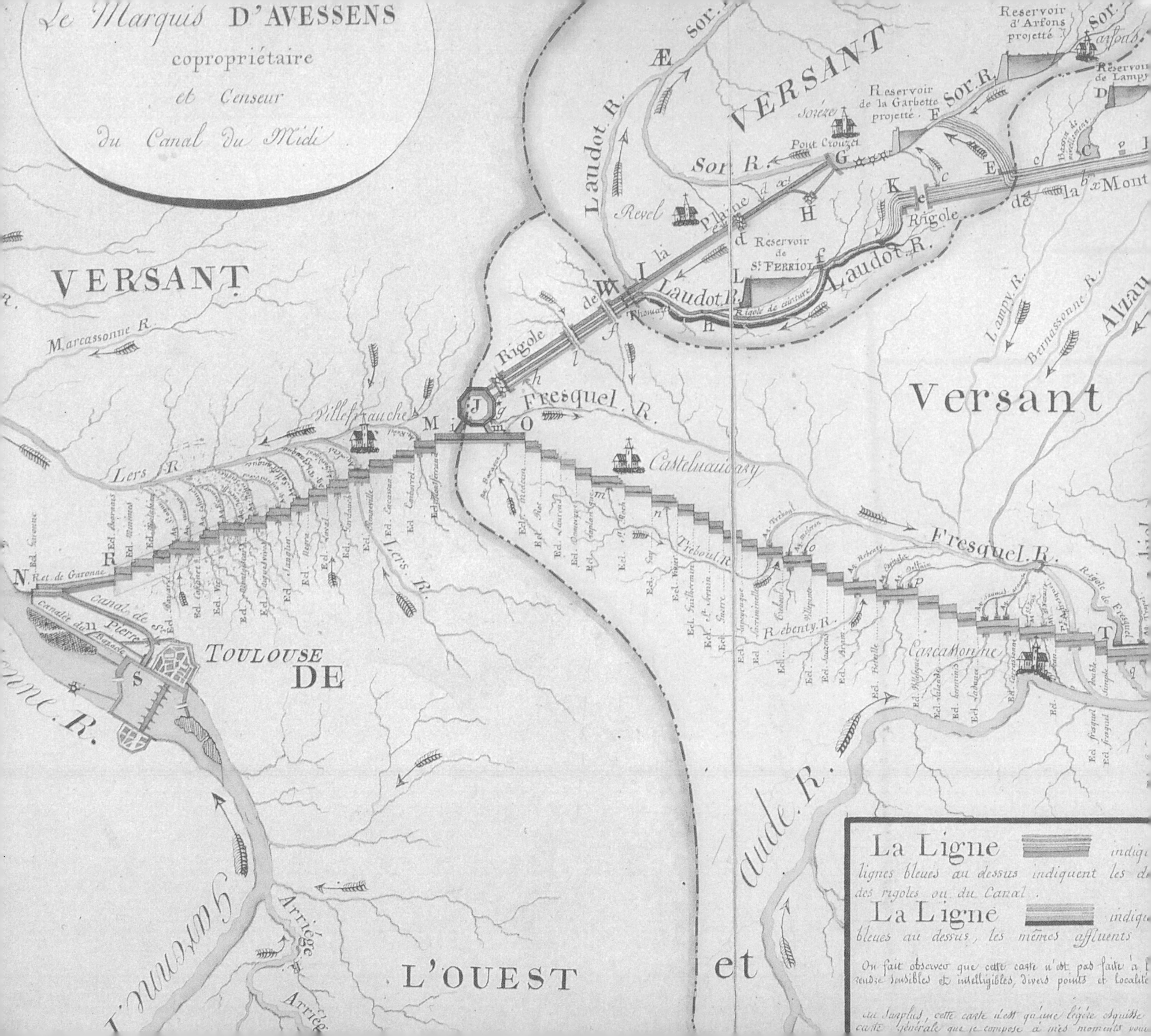
Le Marquis D'AVESSENS
copropriétaire
et Censeur
du Canal du Midi
VERSANT
Versant
VERSANT
DE
L'OUEST
et
TOULOUSE
Revel
Castelnaudary
Carcassonne
Villefranche
Soréze
Reservoir d'Arfons projetté
Reservoir de Lampy
Reservoir de la Garbette projetté
Reservoir de St. FERRIOL
Pont Crouzet
Rigole de la Plaine
Rigole de la Montagne
Rigole de ceinture
Laudot R.
Sor R.
Lers R.
Fresquel R.
Marcassonne R.
Lampy R.
Bernassonne R.
Tréboul R.
Rebenty R.
Aude R.
Garonne R.
Arriége
Canal de St. Pierre
Ret. de Garonne
La Ligne
lignes bleues au dessus indiquent les
des rigoles ou du Canal.
La Ligne
bleues au dessus, les mêmes affluents
On fait observer que cette carte n'est pas faite à
rendre sensibles et intelligibles, divers points et localité
au surplus, cette carte n'est qu'une légère esquisse
carte générale que je compose à mes moments pour